43. Pam, the 'most rural' Mitford, according to John Betjeman.

44. Pam's marriage to Derek Jackson. (*Front row*) Sydney, Derek, Pam, David. (*Second row*) Diana Mosley, Stella Jackson, Nancy Rodd, Aunt Weenie (Dorothy Bailey), Tom Mitford.

45. Debo aged seventeen.

46. David, still prospecting his gold claim in the mid-thirties.

47. Debo and Andrew at their wartime wedding in 1941. David (standing behind Debo, wearing his LDV uniform), broken down by family traumas, 'looked like an old, old man'. (*Left to right, standing*) Sydney, 10th Duke of Devonshire, David, Andrew, 'Billy' Lord Hartington, Duchess of Devonshire.

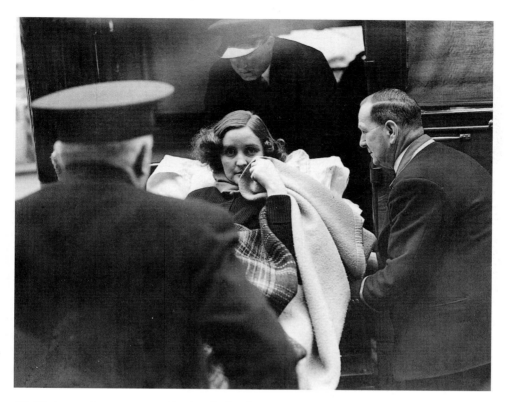

48. Unity on her return to England after her attempted suicide, January 1940.

49. Diana with Alexander on holiday at Inch Kenneth, 1947.

Above left: 50. Nancy, 'the French lady writer' in her Paris apartment. A portrait by Mogens Tvede in 1947.

Above right: 51. Gaston Palewski, Nancy's beloved 'Colonel' and de Gaulle's right-hand man in the Free French Army.

Left: 52. Visit of Princess Elizabeth and Prince Philip to Debo and Andrew at Edensor House (Emma and 'Stoker' in foreground), 1948.

Below: 53. Decca, Dinky and Bob, *c.* 1944.

54. Debo riding Grand National winner Royal Tan at the Devonshire's Irish castle, Lismore, in the mid-fifties.

55. Diana at the Temple, Paris, 1954.

56. Diana and Mosley with their sons Alexander and Max in Venice, 1955.

57. Nancy and Decca at rue Monsieur in 1962.

58. Sydney with her goats at Inch Kenneth *c.* 1958.

59. Diana and Mosley in the early sixties. The body language here says it all.

60. Diana with her youngest son Max; Mosley in the background. London, 1962.

61. Four of the sisters in 1967. (*Left to right*) Cecil Beaton, Nancy, Debo, Pam, Diana and Andrew at a dance after the wedding of Debo and Andrew's son.

62. Decca in front of a plaque commemorating Tom at Swinbrook church. The pews were donated by David, purchased by a win on the Grand National.

63. Bob and Decca at a testimonial dinner in Oakland, 1993.

taken full advantage of that I can hardly blame her I
suppose!). She is beastly about aunts & people who used
to give us huge tips & presents & treats. Diana is outraged
for my mother – I had expected worse to tell the truth –
& of course minds being portrayed as a dumb society
beauty. Altogether there is a coldness about it which I find
unattractive, but of course made up for by the great
funniness.[29]

To Evelyn Waugh, she explained that she couldn't review it:

What I feel is this. In some respects she has seen the
family, quite without knowing it herself, through the eyes
of my books – that is, if she hadn't read them hers would
have been different. She is absolutely unperceptive of my
aunts and uncles, Nanny, and Dr Cheatle [the doctor at
Burford] & the characters whom I didn't describe & who
could have been brought to life but simply were not . . .
Esmond was the most horrible human being I have ever
met . . .[30]

In general, my research for this book tends to support some of
Nancy's comments that Decca *has* exaggerated certain facts.
Some of these are a matter of written record, and others have
been confirmed by a number of surviving family members and
friends who remember how things were at Asthall and
Swinbrook. Decca was distanced from her family for so long, at
a vulnerable time, when she was totally obsessed with Esmond,
and subjected to his critical hard-boiled dislike of them. 'From
what Decca told me,' Bob Treuhaft said, 'Esmond was completely devoid of sentimentality of any kind. I don't know about
a sense of humour, but he would not have understood Decca's
residual fondness for her family. They were "the enemy" . . . It's
quite clear he kept her from visiting Unity.'[31] It appears that

Nancy's myths and half-facts had become genuinely inter-changeable with real memory in Decca's mind. Then, too, she was such a good storyteller and a natural clown, and after telling exaggerated versions of Mitford stories for years to appreciative listeners in California, the jokey versions probably became what she remembered.

Despite this fluttering in the family dovecote, however, *Hons and Rebels* was a resounding hit. Decca showed that she could be as funny, ironic, deft – and waspish – as Nancy, and that she had huge ability as a writer. It seemed that people could not get enough of the eccentric Mitfords, and pre-publication sales in the UK alone netted more than double Decca's advance. As any author with a first book, Decca was nervous about the reviews, but on the whole they were amazingly good. In interviews she enjoyed playing to the gallery, and pulled no punches when asked about Diana: 'I haven't seen her since I was nineteen. We're completely on opposite sides of the fence. Her husband stood for Parliament in the last election and I'm glad to say lost his deposit. His programme was to send all the coloured people to Africa and then divide Africa into two parts, the northern part white and the southern part black. My idea was to form an organisation of "In-laws against Mosley", led by my husband who is Jewish.' Her mother, she told one interviewer, was especially fond of her because, unlike most of her sisters, she had never been divorced or to jail. Her sister Pam, she said, 'used to be married to a jockey'.[32]

With ten thousand dollars assured within a month of US pub-lication, the Treuhafts moved to a new house at 6411 Regent Street, still in the 'old-fashioned neighbourhood' that they so enjoyed in Oakland, but with plenty of space and a garden. At the age of forty, somewhat to her astonishment, Decca found herself successfully launched on a new career with offers flooding in for articles and lectures – *Life* offered her five hundred dollars for five hundred words and *Esquire* offered six hundred dollars for a piece on civil rights in the South. She used the opportunity to go to Montgomery, Alabama, to hear Martin Luther King speak at a Baptist meeting and she became trapped in the church overnight while the Ku Klux Klan and a mob of 1,500 whites hurled tear gas through the open windows. The uproar had been caused by the surprise appearance at the event of the Freedom Fighters, a sort of flying squad of black youths on motorcycles, who were much feared by whites in the Southern states. Next morning when Decca was finally able to leave she found that her car had been burned out. Needless to say the article she turned in after this experience, cleverly titled 'You-all and Non You-all', was rather more controversial and interesting than the one she had originally intended to write.

To achieve a sudden 'respectability' after years of being almost a pariah was a heady experience. She began her second book almost immediately. It was a bit ghoulish, she said, but it had important social connotations. It was about the funeral industry in America and for the next few months she regaled her correspondents with gruesome bits of information on embalming. 'Hen, I'll bet you didn't know what is the best time to start embalming, so I'll tell you: *before life is quite extinct*, according to a text book I've got. They have at you with a long pointed needle . . . with a pump attached.'

In 1961 Debo visited America ('for a *tête-à-tête* with your ruler,' Nancy wrote to Decca); she admired the President a good deal and it was to be the first of five visits she would make to the White House over a couple of years. President Kennedy made one visit to Chatsworth to visit the grave of his sister, as did his brother Robert. Nancy could not resist writing to tell Debo that the *on-dit* at the Venice Lido was that if JFK didn't have sex once a day he got a headache, and to Decca to say, 'Andrew says Kennedy is doing for sex what Eisenhower did for golf.' Andrew had recently been appointed Under-Secretary of State for the Commonwealth. There was a row about this in Parliament since his uncle Harold was Prime Minister. The arch anti-royalist and anti-aristocrat MP Willie Hamilton asked a question about nepotism in the Commons. Macmillan replied blandly, 'I try to make the best appointments I can.'[33]

In the following year Dinky showed that she really did have running-away blood in her, and quit college to work for the civil-rights movement. Decca was furious. She travelled immediately to Sarah Lawrence College, just north of New York, and convinced the Dean to give Dinky, who was regarded as an excellent student, an 'honourable discharge' that would enable her to return to college at a later date. Then mother and daughter, so much alike in many ways, returned to California. 'We were on that train together three days and three nights and we barely spoke a word to each other,' Dinky said. A few months later Decca played at being 'Lord of the Isle' (as suggested by Debo) and went to Inch Kenneth for the first time since becoming its owner. 'Muv was asking me what is to be done with the Isle when she no longer comes here . . .' Decca wrote to Debo from there. 'I said, "Where will you be going?" and she went into gales of laughter, saying, "To the next world I expect." But to my great relief she really doesn't seem to be departing at the moment.'[34] But death was on Decca's mind for she was taking the opportunity to research her book about the funeral industry, she said, and had just come across a fascinating editorial entitled, 'Children's Funerals – a Golden Opportunity to Build Good Will'. 'Do admit, they are a lark,' she wrote.

While Decca was staying with Sydney, Nancy published a little book called *The Water Beetle*. It was a collection of her essays, including a sketch about Blor, the best description we have of the woman who was so important in the lives of the young Mitfords, but Sydney was also portrayed:

My mother has always lived in a dream world of her own and no doubt was even dreamier during her many

pregnancies . . . when she was young she never opened a
book and it is difficult to imagine what her tastes and
occupations [were]. My father and she disliked society, or
thought they did – there again, later they rather took to
it – and literally never went out. She had no cooking or
housework to do. In those days you could be considered
very poor by comparison with other people of the same
sort and yet have five servants . . . Even so she was perhaps
abnormally detached. On one occasion Unity rushed into
the drawing room, where she was at her writing table,
saying, 'Muv, Muv, Decca is standing on the roof – she
says she's going to commit suicide!' 'Oh, poor duck,' said
my mother, 'I hope she won't do anything so terrible,' and
went on writing.[35]

This was the so-called straw-that-broke-the-camel's-back as far as
Sydney was concerned. She and Decca had a blistering row about
Hons and Rebels, the education of the Mitford girls, and Decca
and Nancy's literary portrayal of her as a dilettante mother leaving
the upbringing of her children to nannies. Sydney wrote in a
similar vein to Nancy, deploring the piece. But although Nancy
wrote a conciliatory letter saying that she realized that their education had been the product of received wisdom at the time, rather
than any whim of their parents, Sydney was not to be pacified and
told Nancy what she had already said to Decca: 'I wish only one
thing,' she said firmly, 'that you will exclude me from your books.
I don't mind what you write about me when I am dead, but I do
dislike to see my mad portrait while I am still alive.'

As usual Sydney spent the winter months at the mews. To
save costs, the island was virtually shut down each autumn, the
animals sold off and the house closed except for an occasional
cleaning and airing done by her faithful couple, the McGillvrays.
When she returned to the island in the spring of 1963, she was
accompanied by Madeau Stewart.[36] Madeau, who had trained at

the Royal College of Music, had stayed on the island for weeks at a time over several years and loved being there. 'Sydney played the piano and I played the flute; we used to play Victorian ballads, they were very expressive,' Madeau said. 'And there were lots of books to read and so much to talk about.'

Diana was less enthusiastic about visiting. On one occasion when she travelled back with Sydney they were stuck at Gribun for forty-eight hours in a storm, and finally boarded the *Puffin* in a grey and troubled sea. Sydney, in her eighties, still loved the sea. Wrapped in her oilskins against driving rain and spray, she shouted back to her daughter, 'Great fun, isn't it?' The lack of news, mail and table-talk also bothered Diana, although she conceded that the beauty of the island was some compensation. During those years she and Debo had a pact to write to each other every day while either was on the island, so that they could be sure of at least receiving some mail while they were there. Often the only visitors were picnickers, whom Sydney spotted through binoculars, and she used to send McGillvray as an emissary to invite them to tea. 'Such a haphazard choice of guests was, to me, strange taste,' Diana wrote. 'It must have been the gambler in Muv which made her positively enjoy . . . the luck of the draw at her tea parties.'[37]

About that journey in 1963, Madeau recalled that Sydney was 'very tottery. We had dinner and a bottle of wine on the train, and we got to Oban. I remember there were screams of laughter when I tried to put on her shoes and got them on the wrong feet. Anyway, the crossing was a bit rough and she said she'd like to lie down. That was unusual. When we got to the island she said she wasn't feeling very well and she thought she might call the doctor on Monday.' Alarm bells rang and Madeau decided to get the doctor immediately. She sent for Dr Flora MacDonald, whom Sydney liked. Dr MacDonald recognized that Sydney's condition was serious: having suffered from Parkinson's disease for many years she was now in the terminal stages of the illness and her condition was deteriorating rapidly. Madeau alerted the sisters, and Nancy, Pam and Diana came rushing up to the island. Debo could not leave immediately but Nancy kept her up to date until she could join them. Two nurses came in to help them with round-the-clock nursing, and though there were several periods when it seemed that Sydney was fading she rallied each time. Curiously, for she had been very deaf for some years, her hearing returned in the last days: they kept a fire burning in her room and she could hear the logs crackling and spitting.

'It is so poignant,' Nancy wrote to old Swinbrook-sewer Mark Ogilvie-Grant. 'She feels so ill . . . two days ago she said, "Who knows – perhaps Tom and Bobo?" . . . She laughs as she always has . . . We long for her to go in her sleep, quietly.'[38] A week later Sydney had a minor stroke and slipped into unconsciousness. 'Before that it was dreadful,' Nancy wrote. Sydney had been unable to swallow anything but sips of liquid because of throat constriction and was starving to death. Nancy had often claimed that she had never loved her mother but now she found that her feelings for her were stronger than she had suspected. 'Now she is slipping away and feels nothing . . . the sadness comes and goes in waves. I have a feeling nothing really nice will ever happen again in my life. Things will just go from bad to worse, leading to old age and death.'[39]

Sydney died on 25 May, just after her eighty-third birthday. A carpenter travelled over to the island and made her coffin, and a neighbour said prayers over her body. After a period of fearful storms there was a sudden calm, enabling the coffin to be ferried across to Mull as the sun was setting. The *Puffin*, flying her ensign at half-mast, was escorted by a small flotilla of local boats, and a lone piper played a lament during the short journey over to Gribun. Friends Sydney had known for many years met them and carried the coffin from the little launch to its overnight resting place before it was driven down to Swinbrook. It was all very moving, Pam wrote to Decca. Sydney had wanted to be buried

next to David at Swinbrook where, on what was the first warm
day of spring, the Mitford clan gathered. Debo wrote,

> Swinbrook looked perfectly magical. The birds singing so
> loud, and the churchyard was full of cow parsley and
> brilliant green grass. The sight of Choops,* Mabel . . . and
> all the aunts, so ancient now, and Honks [Diana], Woman
> and Nancy in deepest black . . . the feel of the pews, not
> to mention the taste when licked (do you remember) . . .
> When 'Holy, Holy, Holy' started Honks and I were done
> for; it was too much. We had 'Jerusalem', as well.
> Afterwards we thought we ought to have had 'For Those
> in Peril on the Sea' . . . Hen it was all fearfully upsetting
> and sad. The beauty of the place and the day and the
> flooding memories of that church and village . . .[40]

Decca, who was inexpressibly sad, for in latter years she had
learned to value her relationship with Sydney, sent a subdued
answer: 'I should have felt very lonely if it hadn't been for your
letters (and Nancy's) . . . Thanks *so* much for sending flowers
from me. (By the way my new book is all about the ridiculous
waste of money on funeral flowers and an attack on the Florist
Industry for inducing people to send flowers. But I can see not,
in this case).' Decca was nothing if not irreverent.

In the aftermath of the funeral another Mitford story emerged.
Weenie and Geoffrey were the only survivors of Tap's four children as George had died before Sydney. ('What did he die of?'
Decca had enquired. 'A nasty pain,' Sydney replied.) When she
returned to London from Swinbrook Weenie telephoned
Geoffrey. 'George is gone and now Sydney is dead, don't you
think we should meet?' 'But we *have* met,' he replied, puzzled.[41]

---

*Their old groom, Hooper.

That summer Dinky was invited to Chatsworth for the wedding of Emma (Debo's eldest child) to Toby Tennant, the youngest son of Lord Glenconner. To Dinky's horror everyone kept telling her she looked just like Diana, a compliment in any other branch of the Mitford family but Decca's. 'Silence was the only possible response,' she decided. Like Bob, she was unsure of herself in the big house, though not overawed; if anything her reaction was one of amusement. Invisible hands unpacked her luggage and her laundry was whisked away and reappeared looking fresh and new. 'They keep referring to Kennedy as Jack,' she wrote to her parents, 'and there is an autographed portrait of him in Debo's drawing room.' She found Nancy 'cold and aloof' and Diana 'trying to pretend there was no reason for there to be any unfriendliness between us'. Pam was 'relaxed and ordinary' and Debo 'so sensitive and welcoming'. In an odd sense, because she knew so much about the sisters, she felt like one of them, rather than a niece.[42] By the end of her trip she had reassessed some of her first impressions and thought Pam somewhat uninteresting, but she felt sorry for the way the sisters teased her, constantly making fun of her lack of sophistication and 'basic non-fascination'. Dinky thought this 'cruel – it was as though Pam came from a different family from the rest of you,' she told Decca. She was scared of Nancy at first until she realized that she was meant to be scared: it was Nancy's shell. Andrew's sister told her later that Nancy was actually quite shy.

Decca's book on the funeral industry was published in the summer of 1963; she had worked on it, on and off, for five years. It was Bob who had sparked her interest initially, before the publication of *Hons and Rebels*. He handled the estates of trade-union members and noticed, to his great irritation, that the hard-fought-for union death benefit, intended for widows, often end up in the coffers of undertakers. It didn't seem to matter whether the benefit was a thousand or three thousand dollars, the amount always seemed to be the exact cost of the funeral. As part of his job he attended fortnightly meetings of the local Funeral Society and Decca used to tease, 'Off to meet your fellow necrophilists again?' Having made a few enquiries he suspected that funeral directors used the natural distress of the widows, and their desire to 'do something' for the loved one, by persuading them into buying caskets, flowers and services they could not afford and which, in normal circumstances, they would probably not have considered. Decca, in sore need of a cause and sensing here not just one underdog but a whole pack, took up the matter with alacrity and began her lengthy research. Later she would say that at her age it was easier to sit down at the typewriter and work at being a rebel than going out into the streets and getting her head beaten in by police. An article, which she provoked, was published in the *Saturday Evening Post* in the late fifties, titled 'Can You Afford to Die?' It brought in more mail than any other in the magazine's long and distinguished history.

Realizing from this reaction that there was probably a good book in the subject, she had initially contacted James McGibbon and her American publisher, and suggested that she and Bob would write it. The book was commissioned, but on the condition that it appeared as a work by Jessica Mitford not a joint work on the grounds that 'co-signed works' never sold as well as one by a single author. Bob was a practical man and had no literary ambitions, having already achieved a successful reputation built on his legal career. However, he took a leave of absence from his law firm to work with Decca since the project was so huge and Decca did not feel she could cope with it alone. They shared the research: Bob went off to the San Francisco College of Mortuary Science to learn about the technical side of the industry, such as embalming processes. Decca posed as an about-to-be-bereaved relative with a limited budget, and set out to find how the industry operated in general terms. She was fascinated to see how she could be talked up from the cheapest pine coffin to an elaborate bronze casket, from simple flowers to great floral tributes, to embalming, even when there were no facilities for the family to view the dead body, the hundreds of extras such as Ko-zee shoes (open at the back to allow them to be fitted easily) and cosmetic enhancements. One young sales-man advised Decca seriously that they recommended silk for the coffin lining, 'because we find rayon so irritating to the skin'. A grieving widow who absolutely insisted on the least expensive casket was told, 'Oh, all right, we'll use the Redwood, but we'll have to cut off his feet.'[43]

Nothing was too grisly, sacred or funny for Decca: the cost of dying, she said, was rising faster than the cost of living. Her investigation was savagely incisive and for half a decade she rol-licked through funeral parlours opening wide her large blue eyes and asking innocently droll questions that trapped her victims like flies on sticky paper, without their even realizing they'd been had. She used her family as unpaid researchers in England and France, sending them questionnaires to answer about their expe-riences of funerals. Debo complied willingly, but Nancy balked, writing to explain that she was unable to call on the local *pompes funèbre*. 'I walk past there every day,' she said, 'but I fear I have the superstitious feeling of an old horse passing a knacker's yard.'[44]

Bob also shared the writing process, and the couple had tremendous fun choosing the title, oscillating between such gems as 'The High Cost of Leaving', 'Remains to be Seen' and 'A Funny Thing Happened on the Way to the Mausoleum'. Eventually they settled on the harder-hitting *The American Way of Death*, and despite its subject the book soared effortlessly to number one in the bestseller charts, as Decca's savage yet hilari-ous analysis of the practices of America's funeral industry both shocked and struck chords with the public. Decca dedicated the book to Bob, 'with much gratitude for his untiring collabora-tion', and it earned her a place in a publication called *Women Who Shook the World*.

The American Way of Death was a publishing phenomenon, holding the number-one position in the bestseller charts for months. The publishers were amazed, and so were Decca and Bob. But it was not simply a well-written and interesting read: it made a genuine impact on the way in which Americans regarded funerals. So much so that when President Kennedy was assassinated in November that year, Robert Kennedy chose the least expensive classically designed coffin on offer for his brother's funeral because he had read *The American Way of Death* and had been impressed by what Decca had to say.[45] 'Of all my writings,' Decca once said in interview, 'I'm most proud of *The American Way of Death.*'

Within the first year the book had netted over a hundred thousand dollars in royalties. From now on, like Nancy, Jessica Mitford was a media personality. That is not to say she was popular with everyone: America's funeral industry regarded her as a sort of Lucifer sent to torment them, and they paid her the compliment of referring to her simply as 'Jessica' in their trade papers. They made strenuous attempts to damage her credibility by dredging up her political affiliations, intimating that by damaging the funeral industry she was helping to destroy the American way of life, that she was trying to substitute the American funeral service 'with that practised in Communist countries such as the Soviet Union'. But too many people had been stung and there was enormous support for her demand that some federal controls be instigated to protect vulnerable people. To her amusement Decca found that clergymen were among her staunchest supporters in this.[46]

In the years that followed Decca took on other crusades, such as the Famous Writer School, which advertised for new members with the slogan, 'Would you like to become a writer?' and asked large up-front fees for tuition by mail. Although this was a publicly traded company Decca soon saw off the organization, pointing out in articles, interviews and lectures that so far it had pulled in millions of dollars from students without creating one famous writer. A chic Manhattan restaurant, which added a service charge to a bill she considered already inflated, was demolished in one of her articles. When she investigated pornography she described at a lecture a film she and Bob had watched during research: 'There was a man with an enormous penis perched on a motorbike with a woman. I said to Bob, "That looks dangerous."' A follow-up book, *The American Way of Birth*, spotlighted the huge cost of giving birth. Her signal failure, she thought, was a book about the American prison service: *Kind and Usual Punishment.* She felt strongly about the many injustices she had discovered during this research and, indeed, she made some progress in restricting the use of convicts by drug companies for experimental research. But the book did not sell in huge numbers, perhaps because the book-buying public did not personally associate with the subject as they had with death and birth. But Decca loved taking on controversial topics that no one else would touch and there was no matter into which she would not delve, from racism to venereal disease to the 'sale' of honorary college degrees.

In *Poison Penmanship – The Gentle Art of Muck-raking*, she wrote that in her repertoire she had something to offend everyone. The title was chosen after she was told by a television interviewer that an opponent had referred to her as 'the Queen of Muck-rakers'. She replied, 'If you're going to be a muck-raker it's best to be a queen, don't you think? . . . Of course, the whole point of muck-raking, apart from all the jokes, is to try to do something about what you've been writing about. You may not be able to change the world but at least you can embarrass the guilty.' Afterwards she rushed to the library to look up 'muck-raker' in the *Oxford English Dictionary*. It said 'often made to refer generally to a depraved interest in what is morally "unsavoury" or scandalous', and Decca concluded comfortably, 'Yes, I fear that does rather describe me.'[47]

21

VIEWS AND REVIEWS
(1966–80)

Decca and Bob visited Europe regularly throughout the sixties and seventies, Decca travelling over at least once a year, either with Bob or on more extended trips without him. Before Benjamin left school he often accompanied her on tours of Italy, Spain and France, the pair making an eclectic set of new friends as they travelled. By the end of the decade Benjamin had grown up and started work as a piano tuner. Dinky, who spent the 1960s and 1970s working for the civil-rights movement, parted from the Black Power leader James Forman, by whom she had two sons, and became an emergency nurse working in hospitals in Detroit, New York and Atlanta. To Decca's satisfaction Dinky was to remarry very happily.[1] There was no time in her busy life for her to accompany her mother, so Decca often travelled to Europe alone, but was seldom lonely.

In Paris Nancy took her to Society parties where she revived old friendships with Derek Jackson and others, including, to her amusement, Mr Whitfield, the former consul at Bayonne who had attended her and Esmond's wedding, and in London among leftist literary circles she made new contacts such as Sonia Orwell, widow of George, who became an important friend to her over the next two decades. Nancy insisted on taking Decca to Dior where she introduced her to the *vendeuse* as her 'very rich sister'. For years Decca had quipped that Nancy was dressed by Dior while she was dressed by J.C. Penney, but on this occasion 'I ended up with a dress that cost seven hundred dollars,' she said. Twenty years later she was still wearing it. Occasionally she saw Pam, who made her laugh by threatening to write a book based on the papers she had saved from her years with Derek, since she noted that Decca and Nancy had become 'so rich' by cashing in their memories. Sometimes she stayed with Debo in Ireland or at Chatsworth, or with Desmond, Diana's second son, of whom she and Bob became very fond. Still, she could never bring herself to see Diana and would go out for the day if Diana happened to be calling wherever she was staying. Nancy teased her by telling her that Diana habitually wore a baroque brooch that Decca had given her before eloping with Esmond. 'She says it is her great treasure . . . I hope your hard heart is touched! Sisters, Susan, Ah Soo!?![2] (Confusingly Nancy and Decca always called each other Susan in their correspondence. No one can remember why.)

The downside of these enjoyable trips for Decca was being parted from Bob. She missed the laughter she shared with him, and he was equally affected by their partings. 'Never, never will I let you leave again,' he wrote typically. 'The days drag on and on and it's not even June. Oh Dec I miss you . . .'[3]

In 1966 Bob ran for the office of District Attorney in Alameda County. He knew from the start that he would not be elected, no one with a past rooted in Communism could be, and he was also the first person to challenge the incumbent for fourteen years ('Clear the way with a new DA'). But he received a creditable share of the vote, which was a tribute to his personal local popularity.

As their lives became busier the Treuhafts decided that they had no time to use or look after the island, and put it on the market. Before they sold it, however, they spent a month there, celebrating Bob's fiftieth birthday with a day-long party attended by scores of visitors, including Sydney's old neighbours from Gribun, and Philip Toynbee and Rudbin. The crew of a yacht who put in to get fresh water were bemused to find numbers of jolly people in party clothes (and some in their cups) wandering around the tiny island. Philip Toynbee greeted them: 'If you decided to kill your children because of nuclear attack how would you do it?' he asked, with the careful enunciation of one who had imbibed generously.[4] In the evening there were Highland dancing and parlour games, such as Scrabble, until guests reeled off to bed in the small hours. Two of them decided to swap partners but were discovered *in flagrante*. 'Next morning there was a bit of a frost,' Decca reported to a friend in California. 'Only the innocent really enjoyed the usual kipper.'

The island was finally sold in 1966, and Decca visited for 'one last look' in the following summer. While in London she was introduced to Maya Angelou at a party at Sonia Orwell's home. Maya had just finished writing her bestselling memoir *I Know Why the Caged Bird Sings*, and in the following days she brought sections of the manuscript for Decca to read. The two women were to become the closest of friends, and Bob stated that one of the greatest moments in Decca's life came when Maya began calling her 'Sister'. Decca knew a thing or two about sisters. At about this time she was contacted by a friend of mine, *Sunday Times* journalist Brigid Keenan, who was writing a piece on Nancy and wanted Decca to comment on Nancy's statement that 'Sisters are a shield against life's cruel adversity.' Decca replied, 'But sisters ARE life's cruel adversity!'[5] Her relationship with Maya, however, was supremely important to her. 'It was as close – or closer – than a blood relationship . . . As sisters they went through many good and bad times together,' Bob said, 'and I was sometimes lucky enough to join in.'

While Decca's career was taking off during the last half of the

1960s, Nancy's life was also changing. Fretful in Paris, now that she saw so little of the Colonel, she decided to move from rue Monsieur. She found a house in Versailles, at 4 rue d'Artois, which suited. It was small but it had half an acre of garden, which enchanted her; she thought it was like living in the country. She hated the idea of a lawn and wanted only roses and wild flowers – poppies, valerian, irises, orchids, buttercups, marsh marrow, daisies and harebells. The effect she wished to create was a '*champ fleuri*' and, indeed, in the spring it resembled a country bower: 'My garden looks as though 1,000 Edwardian hats had fallen into it (roses).' By midsummer, however, it was more like an overgrown hayfield. She had as pets a cat, a hen bought for market who won her affection, and a tortoise who crawled out from under the shrubbery in the spring. She spent a lot of time in the garden watching hedgehogs and birds, bees and butterflies. The Colonel visited her sometimes, always her happiest days.

It was on a day in March 1969 that Nancy's world came apart. When the Colonel called to see her he gave her the worst possible news. Knowing how upset she would be, Palewski had found it difficult to tell her he was getting married – indeed, he had called twice and left without broaching the subject because she was feeling unwell. But at last he had to tell her: for on the following day the marriage was to be announced in *Figaro*. Nancy knew his bride quite well: she was rich and titled, and Palewski had been in love with her for many years but her husband had refused to give her a divorce. That alone was a deep wound; for one of the most frequent excuses Palewski had used when Nancy had asked him about marriage was that he could not afford to marry a divorcée without ruining his career. Now he had retired from politics, and he had chosen a divorcée after all, but not Nancy. The newly-weds were to live in the bride's chateau, Le Marais, forty kilometres outside Paris and regarded by many as one of the most beautiful chateaux in France. To her friends Nancy was matter-of-fact in announcing the news ('The Colonel (married) has just been. He makes that face – "it's all too silly" . . .'),[6] as though she had known about it all along and was pleased for him, but the hurt was like a knife.

Shortly afterwards she became seriously ill. Later, she made the link between the terrible shock of learning about the Colonel's marriage and the real onset of her illness, although it is clear that she was unwell weeks before Palewski broke his news. It began with obscure back pains that were written off as lumbago. When the discomfort persisted for two months, doctors investigated and found a lump in her liver. A tumour the size of a grapefruit was removed, and doctors advised Debo and Diana that it was malignant. Nancy was not told of this, as everyone thought it would be too much for her to bear, although when Decca heard, she strongly disagreed. 'I feel it is verging on wicked not to tell Nancy,' she wrote, 'because don't you see, it's awful enough to get such news when one is feeling fairly OK & strong; but if delivered very late in the thing and in much pain, harder to bear I think.'[7] She wrote immediately to Nancy offering to fly to Paris as soon as she could get a flight, and received an enthusiastic reply dated 9 May, which said, 'Oh yes, *do* come.' Decca postponed a planned holiday with Bob in the South and booked her flight. Next day a letter, dated 10 May, arrived in which Nancy said, 'I'm afraid it will be so dull for you as I want to work.' The following day, a further letter, dated 11 May, said point-blank that Decca should not bother: 'My maid is too tired to cope with visitors and I want to work . . . and please don't offer to help [with the housework] as there's no point.'[8] Decca was not only hurt by the apparent rejection but did not know what to do. Then it occurred to her that Nancy's indecision might be related to Diana, who called in on her each day: perhaps the problem of how to keep them apart was worrying her, or perhaps fear about the fall-out when these two estranged sisters met again – as Decca recognized was inevitable.

She consulted Debo, who advised her to go a little later in the year, and Decca did so, after writing that she would be careful to avoid any friction with Diana and hoped Diana would agree. Diana, of course, as mentioned earlier, had made several attempts over the years to reconcile with Decca, all rejected. Decca stayed at a small hotel round the corner from Nancy's house and spent her days sitting with Nancy, trying to entertain her when she was awake. When Diana called in, Decca usually went off to do the daily shopping or performed small tasks to keep out of the way. She spent hours 'removing whole continents of clover from the beds of parsley and lettuce, or anything Nancy asks. Thus I feel useful, in fact indispensable,' she wrote to Bob. There were times, though, when she and Diana were alone together when Nancy was sleeping after an injection. And Decca was usually scrupulous to be well behaved, as she had promised, for Nancy's sake. It was curious, meeting Diana again after thirty-four years: 'She looks like a beautiful bit of aging sculpture (is fifty-nine), they don't have this thing of wanting to look young here, her hair is almost white, no makeup, marvellous figure, same large, perfect face and huge eyes,' she wrote to Pele de Lappe. 'We don't of course talk about anything but the parsley weeding and Nancy's illness. God, it's odd. I thought it must have given her a nasty turn to see me, [I was] aged 18 when last seen by her. But she told Nancy I hadn't changed except for my voice.'[9] Diana's recollection is that they stayed off the subject of politics but often sat on the sofa together, laughing and chatting about the old days quite normally. However, one day while Diana was visiting Decca asked Nancy if there was some little job that needed doing. Nancy asked her to weed a clump of iris and she went off meekly to do so, returning to say mischievously, 'I've given them *Lebensraum*.'* The bitter

---

Lebensraum = 'room to live': Hitler's defence of his attacks on neighbouring countries.

little joke, at which Nancy choked, would not have been lost on Diana, but she did not react and the matter passed quietly.[10]

For a while the worst symptoms retreated and, although it was merely a remission, Nancy thought she had recovered and began work on what was to be another bestselling biography, *Frederick the Great.* The research took her to East Berlin, accompanied by Pam who spoke German, which Nancy did not. There, Nancy had a similar experience to that of Bob and Decca in Hungary: she was approached by a personable young man who told her of his desperate longing for freedom to travel. 'You know, how *can* Decca go on believing in it all?' Nancy wrote to Debo. 'I shall tell her it's all right being a commy in our countries but wait until you are nabbed by the real thing! For ten days we haven't moved without a policeman. I must say it suited me because I loved being looked after . . . still, it's a funny feeling . . . Checkpoint Charlie is *gruesome.*'[11]

Decca was not the only sister to feel concern that Nancy had not been told the truth about her condition: Diana also felt pangs of guilt. 'N. says she has got on so well with the book [*Frederick the Great*] that there is absolutely no hurry . . . this kills one with guilt, in case she reproaches & says I *could* have gone quicker & finished if I'd known.' Her solution was to confide in Nancy's publisher and ask them to press for an earlier delivery date, which worked as Diana had hoped. After the biography Nancy planned to write her autobiography, but the illness overtook her again. For a further three years she suffered increasingly agonizing bouts of illness and pain, offset by shorter and shorter periods of remission. She spent periods in hospital in France and England while her symptoms were investigated until even she suspected cancer, yet despite the malignant tumour the doctors were unable to diagnose the exact nature of her illness so she always had the hope that they would discover the cause and she would be cured. Meanwhile, with each session of illness, the pain grew relentlessly worse. By the time she took up her autobiography it was too severe to allow her to concentrate on writing and she got no further than mentioning it in a few letters to friends and family.

Towards the end she could hardly bear visitors except her sisters, and a few very close friends. Decca went to be with her three times, on each occasion for about a week. Debo and Pam stayed as often as they could, and Diana called almost daily. A few very close friends who could amuse Nancy were allowed to visit, and of course her beloved Colonel. On better days she continued to write her wonderful letters, usually managing to find a joke despite expressions of fearful pain. To her great joy she was awarded the Légion d'Honneur, which was conferred in person by the Colonel. And then, shortly afterwards, she wrote to Decca cheerily:

> It's a deep secret until announced but I've been given the CBE [Companion of the British Empire] which is next decoration after Knight or Dame – quite good for a pen pusher . . . I suppose it's sour grapes but I don't think I could have accepted Dame, on account of being called it, but I do see in my little book that Hons need not use it [the initials CBE on an envelope] because Hon is so much higher in the hierarchy, Good . . . But it may be withdrawn. I've had a furious growl from Downing Street saying too many people know. The reason is that Diana Cooper was sitting with me when I got the intimation – of course you can guess the rest!![12]

In mid-June 1973, warned by her sisters that she should spend some time with Nancy before it was too late, Decca made a final trip to Versailles. While desperately anxious to please, she found that being sister-in-residence was no longer the pleasant task it had been on previous visits. In desperate pain a good deal of the time, Nancy had the querulous air of the acutely ill and had fits of complaining about everything Decca did, from organizing her bedpan to arranging the flowers. When reporting to Debo one day Decca's despair at not being able to do anything right was obvious:

> Her eyes filled with tears & she said 'everyone says there are masses of roses in the garden, *why* doesn't anyone bring them up here?' So I said I'll dash and get some . . . and raced back with three more vases. So N, in cuttingest tones said, 'I see your life does not contain much art and grace.' Too true perhaps, but *Hen*! So I got lots more and put 'em round. Nancy: 'I can't think why you didn't get them earlier, you've nothing else to do.' In other words I think she's rather taken against me . . . of course as Diana pointed out, she's not exactly herself, which I do see . . . Isn't it *extraorder* how utterly preoccupied one is with this horror scene, everything else fades such as Watergate, hubby and kids, all one's usual interests.[13]

To Bob she wrote of wishing to be home: 'As you know we've always been slightly arms-length in contrast with Nancy/Debo, Nancy/Diana or even Nancy/Woman, so it's one of those things where, most likely, one can't do anything right . . . it is all deeply depressing – I rather hope to be fired, in fact.'[14] Before she left Nancy told her during a quiet time that she was 'ready to go', and she even pleaded with the doctor, in Decca's presence, to help her die: '*Je veux que vous me dépêcher* [*sic*].'[15]

Nancy died on 30 June 1973. By then Decca was back in California and Debo sent her a telegram. 'By a quirk of time I didn't get it,' Decca replied to her, 'until I'd seen the news in the paper, "Author Nancy Mitford Dies". A chill, yet blank message since the actual mourning for her has been going on so long.' Indeed, those who had loved Nancy could only feel relief for, if ever there was an occasion when the overused expression 'happy release' was apt, Nancy's death was it. She had suffered harrowing torments, and when the condition was finally diagnosed as Hodgkin's disease[16] she was not surprised to be told by her doctors that the pain was known to be one of the worst. 'The very worst is something on your face called *tic douloureux*,' she wrote in her customary jokey way. 'Bags not having that as well!' Her weight had fallen to under seven stone and her nurses had difficulty finding anywhere to inject morphine. Apart from the fact that the injections hurt, she always held off having morphine as long as possible because she dreaded losing control: 'I have got a little spot of grey matter & I don't want to spoil it with drugs or drink or anything else,' she said. 'My horror of drugs is the greatest of all my many prejudices.' But then came the times when she screamed with pain and had to give in; and in the end only morphine, and the quiet ministrations of Pam, with her loving womanly qualities, could really provide comfort. Just as she had with Sydney, it was Pam who saw Nancy through the worst times towards the end. 'Woman [was] such an utter trooper,' Decca wrote. 'Somehow it looked as though she really came into her own re appreciation of her efforts and rare qualities.'[17] One of the last things Nancy said to Debo was that she recalled hunting as a teenager. If there was one thing she would like to have done, she said, it was to have one more day with hounds.

To James Lees-Milne Nancy had written, 'It's very curious, dying, and would have many a droll, amusing & charming side were it not for the pain . . . the doctors will not give one a date, it is so inconvenient they merely say have everything you want (morphia).'[18] And to her beloved Colonel a few days before the end, her last letter: 'I'm truly very ill . . . I suffer as I never imagined possible; the morphine has very little effect and hurts very much as it goes in. I hope and believe I am dying . . . the torture is too great. You cannot imagine . . . I would love to see you.'[19] He did visit her sometimes, and then, on 30 June, while he was

walking his dog, he suddenly had a strong presentiment that he
must go to see her. Although she appeared to be in a coma when
he arrived, she seemed to smile as he took her hand and spoke to
her. The hearing is the last of the senses to fail and it is almost
certain that she was aware of his presence. He was the dearest
person in the world to her. Soon afterwards she slipped away.
'Nancy was the bright star of our youth,' Rudbin wrote to Decca,
'a gay butterfly fluttering through attainable territories – quite
the wrong person to be ill and suffer. A gossamer personality.'[20]
Diana wrote, too, and her short note survives in Decca's papers.
'Darling Decca, I'm staying with Woman. Nancy's funeral was
yesterday. Swinbrook is looking wonderful . . . Debo will send
obit from the *Times*. All love.'

The cremation was in Paris, and Diana took the ashes to
Swinbrook for burial. She encountered typical bureaucracy, and
a few days before the funeral service it looked as though the
ashes would not be released to her in time. With arrangements
already in hand Debo considered using a substitute box and
burying the genuine ashes later. But it all worked out and
Nancy's ashes were duly buried alongside Unity. Later, Pam had
a headstone erected on the grave, bearing the heraldic device
that Nancy had embossed on her writing-paper. It was a little
golden mole, a creature included in the Mitford coat-of-arms.
Unfortunately, Debo wrote to Decca, the mason concerned was
obviously unfamiliar with moles and on the tombstone 'the result
looked more like galloping baby elephants'. The sisters thought
it irritating but, still, *rather* hilarious. Just as they roared when
they heard that Nancy had told someone that her coffin ought to
be 'a Mitford', so that Decca could collect a 10 per cent royalty.
It had been a long-running joke between Nancy and Decca that
the inexpensive basic coffin she recommended was called 'a
Mitford', and that she collected royalties on every one sold.
Decca did not attend the funeral but Debo told her all about
it: 'green and summery . . . pink and yellow roses all over the

grey-yellow stone . . . there were many friends and none of those ghastly people who crowd into Memorial Services'.[21] She sent a photograph of herself, Pam and Diana in 'deepest black', taken, she said, by a reporter hiding behind a wool merchant's gravestone. 'The result is enclosed, of 3 witches to make you scream.' It was one of those unfortunate pictures when all the subjects were caught off guard looking grim, but James Lees-Milne met Pam at a luncheon party shortly afterwards and she was, he wrote in his diary, 'looking more beautiful than words can say. Her face radiates light.'[22]

The middle years of the seventies were busy and fulfilled for Decca, with curious twists of fate intervening to change the direction of her life. One morning, to her gratified amazement, she opened the mail to find she had been offered the post of 'Distinguished Professor' by the Department of Sociology at California State University at San José, on the strength of *The American Way of Death*. Initially she did not intend to take up the offer, and was content to send copies of the letter triumphantly to her family and friends, but the more she thought about it, the more attractive it sounded. She was offered an honorarium of ten thousand dollars and a faculty house on campus to lecture to 'a small class of honours and/or graduate students' between the end of September 1973 and the end of January 1974. 'We seem to be in a period of rather active intellectual ferment,' the chairman said seductively, 'which I suspect would be as exciting to you as it is to us.'[23]

Decca took on the task with her customary *élan* and within days had clashed with the university authorities for describing the college's loyalty oath as 'obnoxious, silly and demeaning'. Her refusal to have her fingerprints taken 'for records' became a *cause célèbre* when she instigated proceedings against the university after being told that she either gave her fingerprints or faced being locked out of classes. Her lectures were oversubscribed by many times and two hundred students showed up for the first

one in a room designed for thirty-five. Though she treated the
responsibility seriously her droll manner kept the students in
stitches and she made her points as though regaling dinner guests
with anecdotes. Deemed a huge success, despite the 'ruckus' over
fingerprinting, her time at San José University led to other short-
term academic contracts, including periods at Yale and Harvard.
In 1974 she was awarded an honorary degree as Doctor of Letters
by Smith College. This entitled her, she learned, to the letters D.
Litt after her name. 'Wouldn't Muv be amazed to find that Little
D. has been transformed into D. Litt?' she wrote to her sisters.

During a trip to Europe after the term at Yale, Decca and Bob
spent a few nights at Debo's Lismore Castle. 'Bob's face when the
butler came to the door to ask "Shall I lay out your clothes, sir?"'
she wrote to Pele de Lappe, 'was worth the detour, as the *Guide
Michelin* would say.' Debo tried hard to bring about reconcilia-
tion between Decca and Diana, but Decca felt she could not
oblige: 'It's not exactly politics now (except for the feeling one
must draw the line somewhere, and you know all that part),' she
wrote. 'It's more that having adored her through childhood it
makes it 10 times more difficult to have just casual meetings . . .
Even our meetings over Nancy's illness (in which Diana was
marvellous) were rather agony.'[24]

Still, apart from the coldness between Decca and Diana, the
four surviving sisters were closer in the early seventies than they
had been at any time since before the war. This happy state was
brought to an abrupt end by a biography of Unity, written by
David Pryce-Jones, whose father had been a 'what-a-setter' of the
old Swinbrook days. Pryce-Jones had written several books,
which Decca respected, and he had done a good interview with
Nancy. He and the Treuhafts swapped homes one summer, when
it suited Decca to have a long-term London base, and his interest was piqued by the items of Mitford memorabilia he saw
lying around in the Oakland house, 'some of the Acton drawings
of the sisters . . . Coronation chairs with blue velvet seats and the

royal monogram, and Lady Redesdale's set of Luneville china'.[25] A copy of *Jew Süss* with Unity's signature and the date June 1930 especially intrigued him. Subsequently he approached Decca suggesting that he write a biography of Unity, and she gave him what she said was a noncommittal reply, but which he took to be her approval. 'It's not quite like that,' Decca told Debo later, 'I told him that while I was not averse to his having a go at it, the other sisters might be. And that I thought it would be hopeless to try to do it in the face of family opposition . . . After that I forgot about it.'[26] Debo considered it still too early for a biography of Unity, and that without having known Unity intimately 'he couldn't possibly get the hang of the amazing contradictions of her character, nor her great funniness, nor her oddness. Therefore it would miss the point and be Nazis all the way.'[27]

The biography went ahead, and was published in 1976. Though she wrote to Pryce-Jones saying that she thought the epilogue 'really terrific', Decca refused to allow it to be dedicated to her. Even so, her connection with the author caused a great deal of bother between Decca and her family and Mitford friends in England. Pryce-Jones did a huge amount of new research, tracking down childhood friends, people who had known Unity in Germany in the late thirties, and even medical staff who had nursed her after her attempted suicide. The result, which contained verbatim transcripts of interviews with Unity's German connections, and snippets of information gleaned from cousins and family connections, was poorly received by Unity's loved ones, who tended to blame Decca for its publication. It is true that she helped the author with advice and information, telling him on a number of occasions that he must keep her assistance confidential, as she knew her family would disapprove. She hated the thought of losing contact with her family in England ('I dread losing Debo for ever'), but that rebellious streak still ran strong and she gibed at the fact that Debo had made herself the

'self-appointed arbiter of all that concerned the family (especially as I am three years older than she is)'.[28] But not all the
family information in the book came from Decca. Diana gave
the author a very long interview telling him things of which
Decca had not known. This, he told Decca, led him to believe
that if he worked at it he could make Diana 'an ally'. He under-
estimated Diana. She was never in favour and wrote 'an
extremely hostile review' in *Books and Bookmen.* Several people
made a determined attempt to have publication stopped, the
Devonshires, Lord Harlech and the Mosleys among them. This
rebounded on them for, although undoubtedly upsetting to the
author at the time, it nevertheless gave the book much valuable
pre-release publicity. Diana states that she wrote to fourteen
people who were interviewed and quoted in the book and
received back thirteen replies claiming they had been misquoted.
One interviewee, Paulette Helleu, daughter of the painter, was
prepared to take legal action through French courts.

But the author's claims were only half the problem as far as the
family were concerned. It was what was perceived as Decca's dis-
loyalty that most offended. And when some photographs, which
Pam recalled having last seen in Sydney's photo album, appeared
in the plate section, she wrote to Decca in cold anger: 'I suppose
you gave them to him, you could have asked us first. The
album . . . that Debo always had in her drawing room is missing
and can't be found anywhere. Did you borrow it perhaps, as I
believe you are writing your own life? If so we would all like to
have it back.'[29] Decca was livid and wrote a furious reply, which
put her and Pam on 'non-speakers' for more than a year.

Decca had not provided the pictures, and it is clear from correspondence between her and Pryce-Jones that a cousin had
supplied the items in question from her own collection. When
her immediate anger subsided Decca wrote in hurt tones to
Debo, the only sister with whom she was still in regular contact:
'I don't know where we stand . . . [and] I am terrifically sad to

think that perhaps this means it's curtains for us.' Lots of old
hurts were aired, including the fact that Decca had been totally
excluded from any contact with Harold Acton when he was writing his biography of Nancy (published a year previously). 'He
asked if he could quote from *Hons and Rebels*, & I said of course
and he did, extensively, but only to contradict everything I'd
said. You and Woman were closeted with him . . . but not me. I
admit that at that point a certain stubbornness set in. I mean,
why should you be the final arbiter of everything about the
family?' On and on, the letter went, listing the hurts and slights.
'Not only didn't I steal your photo album, I sent you all the
Muv letters from the island . . .'[30]

Debo was equally upset by the episode. 'For goodness' sake
don't let's quarrel,' she begged. 'Here we are getting old, I couldn't
bear it . . . I suppose what we must do is face the fact that we
are deeply divided in thought about many things, but that
underneath our ties are strong.' Nevertheless, she was deeply
unhappy about the book, and felt she must state her case before
the matter was shelved. She deprecated the Pryce-Jones portrait
of Unity, and like Diana, Pam and the cousins she blamed Decca
for co-operating in its production. Mainly, though, she said, she
was deeply saddened that none of Unity's good qualities were
revealed: 'her huge, bold truthfulness, funniness, generosity, hon-
esty and courage'. She explained that, like Diana, she had been
contacted by many of those interviewed, claiming to have been
misquoted in the book, and particularly offensive, to those who
had sight of the manuscript, had been a claim by one interviewee
that Unity had performed a lewd sexual act. 'How can you, as
Muv's daughter, condone such writing?' Debo asked sadly. In the
event Andrew persuaded the publishers to remove this paragraph
before publication.

An uneasy truce followed with Debo and Decca trying hard in
their correspondence to act as though the accusation of theft of
the scrapbook did not lie between them. Decca visited England

in early December in connection with a television documentary. She and Debo enjoyed a pleasant dinner together but they did not touch on the subject of Unity; nor was the joint letter, which Pam, Debo and Diana sent to *The Times* on the eighteenth of that month, mentioned. The letter alleged that the book was at best an inaccurate picture of Unity, and stated that they held letters from a number of interviewees who claimed to have been misquoted. Also they had Unity's papers, including her diary, to which the author had not had access. Cousin Clementine, daughter of the long-dead Uncle Clement, David's elder brother, now Lady Beit, wrote to Decca to say that the biography, when it was released, 'did not cause as much fuss as the scrapbook! The hysteria about the PJ book was violent and did untold harm to the sisters' cause . . . It was difficult to be objective about the book when it appeared. It was as if Bobo just lay there inert, with mud flying and her tragedy totally misunderstood. The book, for me, started as a quest and turned into a witch hunt and I felt David [Pryce-Jones] grew to hate her . . . I felt he did not want to understand her.'[31]

Perhaps at the heart of the matter was that Decca had long ago crossed an invisible line of behaviour acceptable to her family in England. People of her parents' generation, and even most of her own, lived by a strict code that Decca never accepted, hardly recognized. By running away, by treating her parents as she and Esmond had done, by her active Marxism, by the hurtful, small exaggerations in her book, funny though they were, she had broken this code and although she was still loved and welcomed back, her loyalty was never entirely trusted.

The row rumbled on until, in December 1977, the scrapbook was discovered, unaccountably where it was always supposed to have been, in Debo's drawing room. No one knew how it had been missed in the searches. It was 'very *strange*,' Decca wrote pointedly in answer to Pam's explanation for 'it was the size of a table'. But she also noted that 'there was never a word of

could not bear his elder brother Jonathan. She had not seen him since he was four years old when he offended her by giving the Nazi salute, and when he became chairman of the ultra-conservative Monday Club (1970–72), he was forever branded by her 'a dangerous neo-Nazi'.

Shortly after the row about the Unity biography, Diana published her autobiography, *A Life of Contrasts* – 'the truth,' she teased, 'but not necessarily the whole truth'. It was extensively reviewed, and generally accepted as having been well written, but it was slated all the same. Many reviewers used the same phrase: Lady Mosley, they said, was 'unrepentant'. In the main this referred to the fact that Diana wrote her memories of Hitler, the man she had liked and admired, as though none of the things he did later (and none of the things which he was doing at the time, and which came to light afterwards) had occurred. That subsequent historical perspective did not change her original memories rankled. She did not condone the horrors perpetrated by his regime, but merely stated what her own reactions had been at the time. In turn, she had been offended by the factual inaccuracies published about Hitler by journalists and successive biographers; the fact was, she wrote, that she had observed a charming, cultured man, who did not rant and foam at the mouth (as was frequently claimed), with well-manicured hands (not roughened and nail-bitten), a fastidious man who ate sparingly (rather than the cartoon character who stuffed himself with cream cakes). Her lack of criticism brought fury raging down on her head, and her account of her time in the filthy conditions of Holloway invited the comments that many millions of women were incarcerated in far worse conditions during the war, thanks to Hitler and his supporters. A recent biography of Diana suggests that although the book answered some questions and repaid some recent slights it was substantially a vehicle for continuing the campaign that Diana had waged for the past fifty years: that of supporting and defending Mosley.[33] As every author knows,

controversy never hurts a book and *A Life of Contrasts* sold well.
'Diana's style is better than Nancy's,' James Lees-Milne wrote in
his diary. 'It lacks N's debutante touch, and is confident and
adult.'[34]

Despite the hostility of her reviewers, Diana decided to write
another book and her subject was hardly less controversial. Quite
close to the Mosleys' Temple de la Gloire was the Moulin de la
Tuilerie. Nancy had once considered buying the property when
it was an unrestored old mill, but at the time she could not bear
the thought of moving so far from the Colonel. Subsequently it
was purchased by the Duke and Duchess of Windsor and con-
verted into a sumptuous home. Neighbourly invitations were
exchanged and when the Windsors first went to visit the Mosleys
at the tiny temple, the Duchess said, 'Yes, it's very pretty here,
but where do you *live*?'[35]

The Windsors and Mosleys liked each other and got on
well. Perhaps part of the reason lay in the fact that both couples suffered from a perpetual bad press, and that the lives of
each, despite the happiness of a sound marriage, were tinged
by the underlying waste of unfulfilled promise. The unchari-
table, among whom was Decca, saw it as a natural friendship
'given their mutual support of Hitler', though the Duke of
Windsor's so-called 'support' of Hitler's regime is even now far
from being proven. But it would be surprising if there was no
understanding between two women who had each devoted
her life to supporting a man deprived of what he regarded as
his destiny. Diana regarded the Duke's treatment by the Royal
Family as unfair. It was monstrous, she thought, 'to stop him
doing anything and then to put it about that he was frivolous
and lazy'.[36]

After the Duke's death, when the Duchess had slipped into a
long-term comatose state, Diana's old friend Lord Longford (formerly Frank Pakenham), who was a director of Sidgwick and
Jackson, visited the Mosleys at the Temple. He persuaded Diana

to write a biography of Wallis, to correct the many 'lies' that proliferated about her friend.[37] The result is an interesting review of an enigmatic personality, and could hardly be otherwise for Diana had known the Duchess well at a personal level for some years. But it was roughly treated by many reviewers, and condemned as 'a hagiography', presumably because Diana did not subscribe to bringing down her subject, which more and more seems regarded as an essential part of a biographical study. Present-day Royal researchers, however, see Diana's treatment as an important book in the Windsor canon and it sold a respectable 23,000 copies in hardback.

Decca, predictably, deplored it, and dismissed it in her correspondence as '*Woman's Own* writing'. She always displayed a certain amount of *schadenfreude* when Diana was castigated in the press. In answer to one letter from her, Rudbin replied, 'Actually I'm rather enjoying it and Diana is forgiven all for me by the glorious quote: "Come, come, said Tom's father, at your time of life/You've no long excuse for playing the rake/It is time that you thought, boy, of taking a wife/Why, so it is father: But whose wife shall I take."'[38]

Some years earlier Mosley had been diagnosed with Parkinson's disease. He staved off the worst symptoms longer than is usual because he was so strong and fit, had an agile brain and quick manner. In 1968 he had been the subject of a prestigious *Panorama* programme on BBC Television. Over eight million people tuned in to watch his hour-long interview with James Mossman, at that time a record audience. Throughout his seventies he was always happy to be interviewed on television or radio, to argue his corner, to write articles, and shine at dinner parties, but from his eightieth birthday in 1976 there was a clear deterioration. The drugs he needed to take in increasing doses caused him to fall over from time to time.

James Lees-Milne found Mosley physically frail but in good

spirits when he visited the couple at the Temple in May 1980.
Mosley was now, he wrote in his diary,

> a very old man. Shapeless, bent, blotched cheeks, cracked
> nose, no moustache, and tiny eyes in place of those
> luminous, dilating orbs. I sat with him after dinner on a
> sofa and talked for an hour . . . Sir O has mellowed to the
> extent of never saying anything pejorative about
> anybody . . . I asked boldly if he thought he had made a
> mistake in founding the New Party. He admitted it was
> the worst mistake of his life. [he said] the British do not
> like New Parties . . . that if he had led the Labour
> government he would have kept Edward VIII on the
> throne. He [the King] was eminently suited to be an
> intermediary between his country and the dictators. Said
> that critics of himself and Duke of Windsor never made
> allowances for the fact that they detested war, having
> experienced the horrors of the trenches. They wanted to
> avoid it happening again at all costs . . . He stands
> unsteadily, but assured me his head was all right. Held me
> by both hands and said I must come again. 'Why not
> come tomorrow? Come and stay.' Charming he was.[39]

It was the last time Lees-Milne saw him. Mosley died quietly and
suddenly in bed in November 1980.

For Diana it was as though her own life had come to an end.
She had been utterly devoted to Mosley during the whole of
their forty-four years of marriage and now her family wondered
how she would ever cope without him. And though it was a
shock, in a sense they were not surprised when Diana suffered
what appeared to be a stroke and partial paralysis within a year of
Mosley's death.

Further investigation proved that it had not been a stroke,
but a brain tumour, and just as Nancy linked the trauma of the

Colonel's marriage to the development of her cancer, Diana suspected that the development of the tumour in her brain was connected with her devastation at losing Mosley.[40] It was thought that she could not survive. She was flown to a hospital in London where the tumour was confirmed and an operation was scheduled to remove it. 'Oh, hen,' Debo wrote tearfully to Decca, 'she is a person one thought nothing could ever happen to. A rock like figure in my life and lots of other people's.'

Against all the odds – Diana was seventy-one and frail after Mosley's death – the surgery was a complete success. Her paralysis gradually diminished and she was able to get about. Visitors to nearby wards were startled by the shrieks and roars of laughter that emanated from her room as a constant trickle of old friends dropped in to keep her company. It was a reminder of the words of her former wardress at Holloway to a journalist: 'We've never had such laughs since Lady Mosley left.' Her doctor thought at one point that she might be hysterical and ought to be watched. But it was just typical Diana; like her sisters, she is simply so inherently funny that it is impossible not to be amused by her.

One of her most frequent visitors was Lord Longford, who had become a national figure, known, among other things, for his championship of lost causes in the British prison service. As a director of Sidgwick and Jackson, he was one of Diana's publishers, and he and the Mosleys had been in the habit of meeting for luncheon whenever they all happened to be in London, their political differences put to one side. But Diana was touched by his visits to her in hospital. 'Frank's so faithful, the way he comes all the time,' she told her son. And she paused for a moment, before adding, 'Of course he thinks I'm Myra Hindley.'[41]

22

RELATIVELY CALM
WATERS

(1980–2000)

After Nancy's death Decca remained implacable towards Diana, her antagonism too ingrained for her to make any concessions. Throughout the 1980s and early 1990s, the tenor of all the sisters' lives was occasionally interrupted by tensions caused either by Decca provoking her sisters to annoyance by something she said or wrote, or by her reacting to something they had said or written to which she objected. One of these was Diana's portrait of Mosley, contained in her book, *Loved Ones*, which she wrote while convalescing at Chatsworth from her brain-tumour operation. However, Decca contented herself with private criticism in her letters and did not break into print about it, out of consideration for Debo.

Decca's career as a journalist was now at its zenith, and she was a regular and respected contributor to organs such as the *Spectator*, the *Observer* and the *New Statesman* in England, and *Esquire*, *Life* and *Vanity Fair* in the USA. In addition she wrote scores of newspaper articles. Her income from her writing was substantial and despite her apparent indifference to it, one of her intellectual friends told me, 'Decca was financially *very* astute.'[1] Like Nancy, she had triumphed over what both sisters regarded as a lack of education, and had made her way in a tough profession with better than average success. An objective reader might be justified in thinking that the sisters placed more value on formal school education than it warranted, for the true test of Sydney's system was surely what her daughters were able to achieve. When the BBC made a documentary about Decca called *The Honourable Rebel*[2] and she was a guest on the BBC Radio programme, *Desert Island Discs*[3] some of her remarks about their parents, and her stories about the family, were again the cause of a temporary coolness between her and her sisters, even though by this time they had more or less come to expect her to be controversial.

Many readers of this book will be familiar with the BBC production *Love in a Cold Climate*, screened in the spring of 2001. But when, in 1980, Julian Jebb made a television documentary about Nancy, called *Nancy Mitford – a Portrait by Her Sisters,* he inadvertently stirred up what he described as a hornets' nest. His programme was intended to coincide with an earlier dramatization based on *Love in a Cold Climate* and *The Pursuit of Love,* and given access to Nancy's (then) unpublished letters he had been fascinated by the two sides of Nancy: her wit, liveliness and genuine warmth which co-existed with snobbery and the malice so often evident in her teases. Jebb interviewed and filmed Debo and Diana together. 'Lady Mosley and the Duchess loved each other, that was clear at once,' he noted. 'It was not immediately apparent how profound, intense and comical is the Duchess's protective instinct for those she loves, who include every member of the family, living or recently dead.'

As for Diana, 'It is hard to convey her charm, even more to defend her politics,' he wrote. 'The latter are neither flaunted nor evaded but when they come up in conversation they are defended or explained with a temperance of language equalled by a gentleness of tone.'[4] He was especially interested that this most beautiful woman was camera-shy. It seems that just as a plain

woman may have a love affair with the camera and appear a rav-
ishing beauty on screen, the reverse can happen too. It is certainly
true that there are few photographs that show Diana's real beauty
in the way that paintings of her do. 'As soon as we began to
film,' he said, 'her face lost all its customary animation and her
replies to my questions came as if from a mask with darting
eyes.' He concluded that she felt trapped by the camera.

He filmed Pam at her home in Gloucestershire in front of the
blue stove that really *was* the colour of her eyes,[5] and on location
at Swinbrook, standing by the River Windrush, reading Nancy's
description of 'Uncle Matthew and the chubb-fuddler'. Then he
flew to California to conduct his interview with Decca. It had
been set up in advance and he took to her warmth and sense of
fun immediately. Things only began to go wrong when she produced a form for him to sign. This made her co-operation
conditional on his including in the programme extracts of a
letter about Tom, written by Nancy in 1968, at the time of the
publication of Mosley's autobiography. 'Have you noted all the
fuss about Sir Os? . . . I'm very cross with him for saying Tud was
a fascist which is untrue though of course Tud was a fearful old
twister & probably was a fascist when with Diana. When with
me he used to mock to any extent how he hated Sir Os no doubt
about that.'[6]

Jebb was taken aback: 'The letter was bound to offend Diana
and might annoy the other sisters,' he wrote in an article for the
Sunday Times in the spring of 1980. 'First I thought it was wrong
of Decca not to have told me this condition before I had travelled
all the way to California . . . second I thought it ironic that the
great upholder of liberal principles should impose what
amounted to censorship, for it is just as restricting to be forced to
include something as it is to be forced to delete it.'[7] In the end,
though, Decca prevailed and he had no option but to include the
letter. Working with Decca, he was struck by her articulate pro-
fessionalism, but also by her 'intense sadness' at her long

separation from Nancy. Diana was not upset, but she insisted on stating during her interview that Tom had been a paid-up member of the BUF, a fact now historically confirmed and curious in view of his pro-Jewish sympathies.

The letter certainly caused more bother between the sisters in private than its inclusion in the programme merited, and following this incident Decca made a trip to England without contacting Debo or Pam. The public, however, was now so inured to the political rivalries of the sisters that the item about Tom failed to have any shock impact. Decca had felt she must make the point about her brother for he had been the only member of the family whom Esmond could bear. When the dust settled she wrote to Debo explaining that she simply didn't believe Tom had been a Fascist. 'Neither, apparently, did Nancy, so I wanted to be sure to get that in.' But it is clear from Tom's own correspondence with his oldest friend, James Lees-Milne (which, of course, Decca would never have seen), that he was sympathetic to Fascism if not Nazism. The real surprise of the programme was seventy-three-year-old Pam, for in it the 'quiet sister' emerged as a star performer. Giggling, pretty, funny and sometimes serious, she positively stole the show from her more famous sisters.

At this point the Mitford industry, as the sisters referred to books and articles about their family, was at its peak, and books, plays and articles proliferated. There was a light-hearted musical called *The Mitford Girls* based on their lives. When Diana, Debo and Pam attended a performance the manager of the theatre gave them badges to wear, which read, 'I really AM a Mitford girl.'[8] One of the most important of the books was arguably Nicholas Mosley's *Rules of the Game*, published in 1982, about his father. Nicholas was Mosley's son by Cimmie, and the book was candid about Mosley's prolific sex life and his mother's distress at his father's infidelity. Among other revelations he included private letters between his parents, written when

Mosley and Diana were lovers in the period leading up to
Cimmie's death. Diana and her Mosley children were outraged,
as were Nicholas's own brother and sister. Diana was motivated
by a fierce protectiveness of the love of her life for whom she was
still grieving. Nicholas' siblings and his half-brothers perhaps
felt they had already suffered enough publicity because of their
father. They all felt it was 'too soon' to make this sensitive
material public.

Nicholas justified the book by explaining that his father had
asked him to write it shortly before he died, and that Diana had
given him the letters without reading them. This surely says a
great deal about Diana, for how many second wives would hand
over this type of correspondence without at least a glance at it out
of curiosity? Max, Mosley's youngest son and Nicholas' half-
brother, suggested that his father was not *compos mentis* when he
gave permission for the book, but Nicholas pointed out that
Diana had been present at the time. Diana attempted to have
publication stopped, but once again the action merely resulted in
publicity, which helped the book. It was hard for Diana to have
this aspect of the personal life of the man she still worshipped
spread out for public consumption, and from a source that gave
it such authenticity. Predictably, Decca rather enjoyed the embar-
rassment caused and made quips about it in her voluminous
correspondence.

A year later Jonathan and Catherine Guinness wrote *The
House of Mitford*, in which the Mosley case was strongly argued.
This time it was Decca who refused to co-operate by withholding
permission for any quotes from *Hons and Rebels*, or indeed any of
her books or letters. 'Leave me out,' she wrote to her nephew
grimly, 'you'll have plenty of copy from the rest of the family.'[9]
Her dislike of Jonathan had been bolstered recently at a meeting
with his daughter Catherine who, when interviewing Decca for
an article, showed her a letter from Jonathan in which he warned
her about Decca:

She's a very tough cookie [he wrote], a hardened and
intelligent Marxist agitator who knows very subtly how to
play on her upper-class background so as to enlist residual
snobbery (on both sides of the Atlantic) in establishing
Marxism. But this leads to problems of identity; to an
ambiguity as to what is real and what is an act. All this
was very evident in her TV appearance here. Bob Treuhaft
came over better, at least he *is* what he is. He is one piece
so to speak, the bright Jewish boy with his ready made
'red diaper' principles, seeing (e.g.) Chatsworth from the
outside with the healthy irony of a social historian.[10]

Decca interpreted this letter as implying that she was 'a liar
and not to be trusted', though Jonathan did not use those words.
One friend of many to whom she wrote about the affair, wisely
counselled her: 'He probably doesn't understand the immensely
important help you have given by instinct and design, to a host
of people, for most of your life, and you will never understand
that the very rich and powerful, in their isolation, also need
succour.'

For fear of alienating Debo again, Decca refused to review
the book for the *Guardian*. Instead, she sent sheets of quotable
material to her circle of literary friends in England for them to
use in their own reviews of the book, which she described privately as 'a puff job for the Mosley faction'. Several reviewers used
extracts from these 'crib sheets' of Decca's, and at least one major
review was copied almost word-for-word from Decca's comments. Decca knew her way about the world of English
reviewing which she described as 'a small pond where people
scratch each other's backs – or bite each other's backs – and they
all know each other. At least in California if your book is
reviewed well you know it's because they like it.'[11]

She employed the same tactics two years later when Selina
Hastings brought out a biography of Nancy. Decca was surprised

to hear that Debo, Pam, Diana and some of their childhood
friends and cousins liked the new portrait of Nancy. But her contemporary letters show that she had taken against the author
even before she read the book, for quite another reason: in writing to Decca, and to a New York newspaper, the author had
signed herself 'Lady Selina Hastings'. This irritated Decca: she
regarded it as snobbish and she was determined not to like the
book. When the biography was published it contained a deroga-
tory remark about Bob (Treuhaft) and as far as Decca was
concerned the gloves were off. She wrote a review, 'Commentary
in Defence of Nancy',[12] which was a brilliant, scathing and, of
course, amusing condemnation of the book, but unfair in that
she based her criticism upon a few selected passages. She made
no reference to the immense amount of fascinating new material
about Nancy's relationship with Palewski, including their private
correspondence, which even Decca privately conceded was
'amazing'. And, even accounting for personal taste, the Hastings
biography was far more incisive than the previous one, written
by Harold Acton shortly after Nancy's death, which Decca found
unsatisfactory. In case they should miss seeing her review, Decca
copied it and sent it to all her Mitford friends and connections,
some of whom – to their credit – wrote to disagree with her
opinion. 'Thank you for sending me your championship of
Nancy,' James Lees-Milne wrote, while also advising that she had
misquoted him in her review. 'The Redesdale motto should be
"Decca Careth For Us", instead of God,* for whom I don't suppose you have much use. And I admire your loyalty but, alas, I'm
afraid we don't yet agree even on [this] book.'[13]

What makes this review, and those Decca wrote of other
books at the time, especially interesting to a biographer is what
it reveals about Decca's tight and confident literary style. For all

*Redesdale motto: *God Careth For Us.*

the success of her first book *Hons and Rebels* (in the opinion of many, including me, her best book) Decca's literary voice then had been that of an apprentice compared to what it was to become. By the 1980s her irreverent flourish had developed a polish that placed her in a superior pantheon as a wordsmith. And although her books after *The American Way of Death* did not have the same massive success, they were generally profitable and, more importantly, because of them, she was in constant demand for nearly two decades as a journalist and speaker. A simple list of her published articles would cover a dozen pages and she never failed to be delighted when offered a huge sum of money for her words.

It was at this point, in the mid-1980s, that I came into contact with her. She was warm, kind, bubbling. In interviews for this book I learned from numbers of people of her generosity to friends in trouble. Indeed, some months after our first contact, when she heard that my partner had died suddenly she was both hugely sympathetic and practical. She was, in fact, pretty well irresistible. This was the side of Decca that her friends saw, but woe betide an enemy. As an opponent Decca transformed herself into a determined avenger, able to use the power of words and her celebrity status as weapons. Her letters to friends are as full of spicy gossip as were Nancy's.

In January 1984 Decca flew to Nicaragua with a group of writers concerned with press censorship there and in neighbouring El Salvador. Within a short time of her arrival she suffered a deep-vein thrombosis while getting into an elevator: 'It was a very odd experience,' she said later, 'first a hand went, then a foot . . .'[14] Fortunately, it was only a minor stroke and within a few months she had recovered and was back to normal, apart from a moderate limp. But it frightened her. For years she had been drinking and smoking heavily – when short of words she found drinking helped, and she had been addicted to cigarettes from her youth. Now, three years short of seventy, these indulgences began to take an inevitable toll. Warned to give up smoking at least, she promised to try, and took to chewing a brand of gum marketed in the USA as an aid to quitting, 'because I have been such a bore to Bob and everyone,' she wrote to Debo. 'He was a total saint this time but how can he be expected to be ditto if it recurs due to my own fault?'

Apart from a few months for recuperation from the stroke, her work was unaffected. Later in 1984 she wrote *Faces of Philip*, an affectionate memoir of Philip Toynbee, Esmond's oldest friend, and she followed this with a biography of her mother's heroine, Grace Darling. Both books required her to spend long periods in England researching, and *Grace Had an English Heart* was eventually published in 1987. Neither of these latter books sold in quantity and Decca became bored with Grace Darling long before she completed the work. 'Grey Starling is about to take wing,' she wrote to her correspondents, 'oh the amazing relief. *Decompression.*' She was far more interested in the fulfilment of a long-held ambition: a trip to Russia.

Bob and Benjamin, along with Dinky, her husband and two children, and her immense circle of friends in the Bay area, many of whom dated back to the days when she had first arrived in California in the early 1940s, were paramount in her life, but she relished any new controversy that reared its head in the news as natural fodder for her articles. In the spring of 1989 the Islamic *fatwa* was declared on Salman Rushdie for his book *Satanic Verses*. On the day this was announced Decca appeared wearing an outsize cardboard lapel badge upon which she had printed 'I *AM* Salman Rushdie'. Later the badge went into production and was worn all over the USA by those opposed to literary censorship, and subsequently Rushdie himself was absorbed into Decca's vast international circle of literary and media friends. 'About the Salman Rushdie badges,' Decca wrote gaily to Debo, 'I'd send you one, but I fear you don't look much like him.'

Some years earlier, in 1982, Debo had also broken into print with *The House*; it was part autobiography and part a contemporary history of Chatsworth. She had written it as a product for the Chatsworth shops but it sold well generally, both in the UK and the USA, and she suddenly found herself touring on the lecture circuit in its wake. 'Nancy once told me,' Decca wrote, 'that if you ever became a writer you'd put us both in the shade.' In response to frequent requests from visitors Debo also wrote *The Estate* in 1990 (and in 2001 was working on a revision of *The House* prior to its planned republication).

When Andrew and Debo celebrated their golden wedding anniversary in 1991, the Duke spoke of their years together: 'My wife and I realize how lucky we have been,' he said. On thinking how best to celebrate the occasion he had had the idea of a 'golden wedding party' to which he and Debo would invite not friends and dignitaries but other Derbyshire couples who had married in 1941. He thought that, with luck, a dozen or so marriages might have survived fifty years and made the announcement. To the Devonshires' surprise and amusement, nearly a thousand couples applied, not all from Derbyshire, and this resulted in a massive party, held in a marquee almost a quarter of a mile long, at Chatsworth. There are undoubtedly some who would dismiss this generous gesture as paternalism, but there is equally no doubt that the happy occasion gave pleasure to a large number of people, and the attitude of the Duke and Duchess towards each other at that event showed the depth of their affection for each other.

In the latter years of the 1980s, Diana and Pam, who was now increasingly lame in the right leg that had been weak since her childhood attack of polio – 'I'm a bit short in the offside leg,' she would say in answer to enquiries – spent a number of holidays together, in Switzerland and Italy in the summer, and several winters in South Africa. They had grown very close in the last decade and enjoyed each other's company. 'I do hate winters now I'm old,' Diana wrote to James Lees-Milne. 'I feel happy in the sun among flowers.'[15]

She had endeavoured, in the absence of Mosley, to fill her life with serenity and beauty, but in November 1989 she provoked national controversy merely by appearing as a guest on *Desert Island Discs*. The BBC had tried to air the programme on three occasions: the first date they chose, 8 October, was changed because someone rang in to say that it was the eve of Yom Kippur, which was surely inappropriate scheduling. It was then announced that the programme would air on 1 October but the schedulers were advised that this was Rosh Hashana (Jewish New Year). A third date announced, 19 November, was found to be the date of the annual memorial parade of Jewish veterans, so the programme was rescheduled for a fourth time to 26 November. To Decca, it did not matter when the programme aired: the mere fact of giving Diana an opportunity to speak in public proved that the BBC was 'deeply imbued with the deep-dyed anti-Semitism that pervades all England'.[16]

As always, Diana answered the presenter's questions frankly, calmly and without hedging or exaggeration. Hitler was, she said, 'extraordinarily fascinating and clever. Naturally. You don't get to be where he was just by being the kind of person people like to think he was . . . Of course, at that moment he was the person who was making the news and therefore he was extremely interesting to talk to.' He had mesmeric blue eyes, she recalled. She had never believed there would be war between England and Germany, 'I thought reason would prevail,' she said. 'Had I the slightest idea I would be imprisoned I would have given up going to Germany. My duty was to be with my children.' She minded very much that she had missed those vital years of her children's lives: they had all changed completely by the time she was released.

According to newspaper reports, many listeners were upset by what appeared to be Diana's defence of Hitler, but Jewish leaders were infuriated by her championship of Mosley. Denying that he was anti-Semitic, she said, 'He really wasn't, you know. He didn't know a Jew from a Gentile . . . But he was attacked so much by Jews both in the newspapers and physically on marches . . . that he picked up the challenge. Then a great number of his followers who really were anti-Semitic joined him because they thought they would fight their old enemy.' Yes, she admitted, he had referred to Jews as 'an alien force which rises to rob us of our heritage' in a speech in 1936. 'One of those things which horrified him,' she said, 'was that we had this enormous Empire and he did think that the Jews, and the City in general, had invested far too much in countries that had nothing to do with our Empire . . . They were attacked by Communists very often on peaceful marches through east London and in all the big cities, and when there is a fight people are injured of course.'[17]

It was undoubtedly insensitive of the BBC to schedule the programme originally so that it coincided with Jewish anniversaries, but equally one senses that the inadvertent clashes of dates merely added another card to the hand of those who opposed the Mosleys, and that Diana would have been attacked, automatically, no matter when the programme went out. A Jewish representative stated, 'The activities of Oswald Mosley in the 1930s were racial, discriminatory and blatantly anti-Semitic. He capitalized on the economic difficulties of the 1930s attempting to throw responsibility on world Jewry . . . There can be no whitewashing Oswald Mosley today . . . BBC listeners should not be exposed to apologia for Hitler and Oswald Mosley.'[18] A BBC statement said that they had received some complaints from Jewish listeners but equally they had received a positive response from people who had enjoyed the programme. Diana had been close to centre stage in world history for a while; therefore, what she had to say was of immense interest.[19]

On 12 April 1994 a devastated Debo telephoned Decca to advise that Pam had died from a blood clot after surgery for a broken leg. Although eighty-six, Pam had continued to lead a full life right to the end, having only to curtail somewhat her beloved trips abroad in recent years. As with her sisters, age had made little difference to the way she lived, thought or wrote, and only physical impossibility prevented her leading the life she had lived since she was a young woman. At her eightieth birthday party she had wowed her guests by appearing in a gold lamé coat, and sat radiant with pleasure, her eyes still that amazing shade of blue, which showed no signs of fading to octogenarian paleness.

The accident occurred during 'a jolly weekend in London'. She had spent the day shopping, and after dinner with friends was invited next door for drinks. Despite her usual care (she had written to Decca a short time earlier advising her to be careful about breaking legs or hips), she fell down some steep steps and suffered a clean fracture below the knee in her weak leg. She was taken to hospital where the bone was successfully pinned, and on coming round from the anaesthetic her first words were 'Who won the Grand National?' Within twenty-four hours she was sitting up in bed entertaining visitors, such as Debo's grand-daughter, Isabel, with her new baby, and several other callers, and being her usual 'terribly funny' self. Debo was in Ireland and spoke to Pam on the phone. She had just arrived in London when she received a message to go directly to the hospital. Pam died ten minutes before Debo could get there.

'But imagine how she, of all people, would loathe a life confined to a wheelchair with somebody to look after her,' Decca wrote. 'And – God forbid, to do the cooking! (how I'd hate to be that somebody, come to think of it).' The last time Decca had seen Pam was in the previous autumn when Decca was a guest speaker at the Cheltenham Literary Festival. She and Bob had taken several people to Pam's cottage ('neat as a pin'), which was near by, and Pam had cooked 'the most delicious 3-course lunch . . . completely single-handed'.[20] The scrapbook row, which Decca had not forgotten but had decided to overlook, was long behind them.

Hosts of friends attended the funeral at Swinbrook to sing the hymn sung at all Mitford funerals, 'Holy, Holy, Holy'. Today, a small oak planted by Pam on the village green is as much a memorial to 'the quiet Mitford sister' as is her headstone in that peaceful place, which held so many childhood memories. Although she had no children of her own Pam's many nieces and nephews were left feeling bereft: 'Tante Femme's' maternal and caring qualities were unique in the family, and of all Sydney's daughters she was the most like her mother. A friend who attended the funeral wrote and told Decca that Debo had forbidden the vicar to preach a sermon – 'So like Farve with his stopwatch set for ten minutes,' Decca commented.

In November that year Decca was staying at Dinky's apartment in New York. She tripped on the hem of her long skirt as she and Bob were leaving to go out to dinner and suffered multiple fractures in her ankle. After a cast was fitted she and Bob were able to fly back to California where she was cared for by Benjamin's Korean wife Jung Min. Decca wrote to Debo that she was well aware that the accident had been caused by clumsiness because she had had too much to drink. She had broken her wrist a year earlier in the same way. She knew she had become far too dependent on alcohol to get her through difficult times, to enjoy good times, and increasingly simply to get her started in the morning. She considered all this and made a decision to give it up, cold turkey.

Dinky was now a highly qualified nurse. At one point she had been appointed a director of the hospital but found she disliked being away from the bedside: her vocation was nursing, not administration. She asked to be returned to nursing, offering her resignation if this could not be arranged, and was subsequently responsible for establishing an acute-pain and palliative-care clinic where she still works. The caring characteristic that Decca had noted in her infant daughter, which had so reminded her of Pam, had never faded, and as a professional Dinky was intensely aware of how difficult it was going to be for Decca to give up drinking. She considered it could not be done without help. 'She drank heavily for years and I do want to mention it because the way in which she gave it up shows the strength of Decca . . . When she tripped on the hem of her skirt she had been drinking and had had too much. It wasn't unusual. She could be very mean when she'd had too much to drink. A different person altogether . . . I never preached to my mother, but she suddenly realized what it was going to mean if she continued drinking as she got older, for example if her drinking caused another stroke . . . she couldn't stand the thought of being alive and dependent.'[21]

Decca confounded Dinky, remaining calm and showing none of the usual symptoms of withdrawal distress. 'She is positively amazing,' Dinky wrote to Maya Angelou. 'She's now [gone] 18 days without a drink. She fired the substance abuse psychiatrist after he droned on about residential treatment, group therapy, AA etc. She just looked at me with her blue, droopy eyes, and said, "I've decided to give it up, that's all."'[22] Dinky said she had never been prouder of her mother than during those early weeks when Decca turned her back on drinking. When she was mobile again, Decca attended AA meetings and Dinky acted as her 'friend'. 'She only ever called me three times,' Dinky said. 'She did it by sheer will-power. Once she gave up drinking she became a different person. A new and softer Decca emerged. All the crossness and meanness disappeared.' Bob agreed with this: it was a return to the old Decca and the Treuhafts' relationship benefited.

Decca's smoking was another matter. She had given up years earlier, ostensibly. While she had even given a series of lectures on 'giving up smoking', her biggest problem during these lectures, she wrote to Debo, was finding the time to run to the ladies' room 'to have a quick puff every now and then'. She chewed nicotine gum at the rate of six packets a day. 'She was so fastidious and it was quite uncharacteristic of her to chew gum,' Bob reflected. He genuinely believed she had given up smoking. One day, however, she was discovered *in flagrante delicto*: 'Dinky caught me and told Bob,' Decca wrote to a friend. 'How *awful* of her . . . So I suppose I will have to give up for real now.' And she did so, though she never got over the craving for cigarettes. 'Oh how I should like a puff,' she wrote wistfully, in letters to her many correspondents.

Now in her mid-seventies Decca kept up a pace that would have punished someone twenty years younger. She was still in demand for lectures and public appearances, even appearing tremulously, on one occasion, side by side with Maya Angelou as they rode two elephants at the head of carnival procession. In June 1996 her broken ankle was giving her trouble; in compensating for it she had thrown out her hip, causing enough pain to make her consult a doctor. She also mentioned to him that she had been coughing blood for a few days. A series of X-rays and blood tests carried out subsequently provided a shock diagnosis: she had lung cancer.

'It's a bit of a facer, Hen,' she wrote to Debo, but she said that she and Bob had decided to go ahead with plans for a holiday in Cape Cod in August. It was a place she had always loved since her time there with Esmond. In recent years she and Bob had visited the resort every summer as guests of Jon Snow, the Channel 4 news anchorman who had become a close friend after helping Decca with some awkward packing after a long visit to London. Decca instantly bestowed upon him the soubriquet 'Packer' Snow. Meanwhile, she said, she was determined to finish her present commission. It was an up-to-date revision of *The American Way of Death* or – as she referred to it in correspondence – 'Death Warmed Up'. She also amused herself by writing to 'Miss Manners', a San Francisco newspaper column on matters of etiquette. Was it, she asked, contrary to the rules of etiquette for a dying person to exploit the pity of their friends to make them do what she wanted?

In July she went into hospital for further tests pending a course of chemotherapy, and the results were even worse than antici-pated. The cancer had spread to her liver, kidneys and brain and was thus inoperable. The doctors recommended her to forget chemotherapy and to have radiation of the brain, to conserve its function for as long as possible. With her years of experience at the highest levels of nursing, Dinky was the family spokesper-son,[23] and though the prognosis was difficult for the rest of Decca's family to take in, it was perhaps worse for Dinky, who knew precisely what it meant, clinically, for her mother. Decca took it in the way she had always taken bad news: on the chin. 'You're so brave, Little D,' Sydney used to say. Even so, Decca asked Dinky to pass on the news to Debo, Maya and the people closest to her. The one thing she had never been able to face was sympathy.

Writing on 11 July to Debo, to thank her for contacting Jon Snow, Decca said, 'The Packer wrote such a funny fax, saying he'd never heard a Duchess say *Bugger* so much . . .' Her situation was curious, she said. She was suffering no headaches or even malaise following the radiation, just some pain in her thigh. Meanwhile life was quite pleasurable with innumerable friends rallying round, bringing in food and gifts, and she was working on the book. Although she had been given a prognosis of only three months, she found it difficult to believe this could be cor-rect and was half convinced that a major mistake had been made in the diagnosis.

There was no mistake. Within days of writing this letter Decca began to suffer paralysis in the right side of her body and was admitted to hospital. Though concerned, when they ascertained that she had not suffered a stroke, the doctors agreed that she could still go to Cape Cod in a few weeks' time. From then on, however, her deterioration was rapid. 'It seems that one of the cancer lesions in the brain may have swollen or bled a bit,' Dinky reported. A week later Decca was being fed through a tube but after a few days she asked for this treatment to be withdrawn. 'Yesterday she told Bob . . . she wants to come home to die,' Dinky advised Debo. 'She looks pale and tired . . . she wakes up and smiles and tries to talk. She's very clear about what she wants, knows who everyone is. Bob asked her if she wants you to come, and she says she doesn't see the point . . . Who could have imagined this would go so fast?'

Decca's last four days were spent at home: her hospital-type bed was installed in the spacious sitting room she loved, surrounded by her books and pictures, Mitford memorabilia, closest friends and members of her family. Maya Angelou came every day and while Decca could still laugh they laughed together. At the end 'Maya was the real doctor,' Bob said. 'Decca was not reacting to anything. She could hardly swallow and barely recognized people. Maya would come in each evening and stand by Decca's bedside and sing to her . . . bawdy songs, romantic songs and Decca would finally react and realize, "Oh, it's you." And she would even open her mouth and try to sing along. Her last words were really songs that Maya started her singing . . . I'll never forget Maya for that. It was one of the great moments of my life learning what true sisterhood is all about.'[24] Decca died on 22 July less than six weeks after being told she had cancer.

Her funeral was minimal. She organized it herself from hospital: a no-frills cremation with her ashes to be scattered at sea, at a total cost of $475. Yet her host of friends wanted to mark the memorial service with something more fitting to her huge personality. Once in an interview she had been asked what sort of funeral she had in mind for herself and she had replied wryly, 'Oh, I'd like six black horses with plumes, and one of those marvellous jobs of embalming that take twenty years off . . . The streets to be blocked off, dignitaries to declaim sobbingly over the flower-smothered bier, proclamations to be issued, that sort of thing . . .' In a remarkable tease on Decca, that is almost what happened at the memorial service. More than five hundred people attended the service at a hall in Delancy Street, San Francisco. Tributes from friends were interspersed with old hymns from Decca's childhood, and the service finished with a band playing 'When The Saints Go Marching In'. As they spilled out on to the street, those who attended were greeted by the sight of six black horses wearing plumes and harnessed to an antique glass hearse that had been drawn up outside the hall. Inside it were copies of all Decca's books and articles.

A few months later there was a memorial service in London. It was held in a theatre, for it would have been hypocritical to hold it in a church, although this is the more usual venue in England. Debo had intended to go, and to speak, but press reports that it was to be 'a circus' with 'sideshows' of funeral directors showing their wares worried her. At the last minute she decided not to attend. However, a huge number of media personalities did go. Packer Snow compèred and Maya Angelou stepped in to pay the main tribute in place of Debo. It was a warm occasion, full of laughter, in celebration of the life of a woman who was brilliant, feisty and surprisingly complicated.

Decca did not live to finish her revision of *The American Way of Death*, but Bob completed and published it, using Decca's notes. 'I tried to preserve as much as possible of Decca's inimitable way of putting things,' he said. He still lives in their family home in the pleasant traditional 'neighbourhood' in Oakland. The house is old-fashioned, shingled, and has a generous front porch. Scented red and white roses planted by Decca flourish by the front steps. At the rear is a small enclosed garden of Californian flora, alive with humming birds, and squirrels scampering across the rails of the decked patio. When I last saw him in October 1999 Bob had just taken delivery of a new computer after organizing a website for Decca's books. 'We've had 1,300 hits already,' he told me gleefully, and gave me some instruction on using e-mail, a technology that I had yet to tackle. 'Decca had no idea of technology,' he recalled, but she had been thrilled by the instant communications provided by her fax machine. Shortly after she started using it she came downstairs on Christmas Eve to find that the messages received overnight had a red border. It did not occur to her that this was a warning that the paper was running low: 'She thought it was a delightful festive touch provided by the manufacturers,' he said, smiling at the memory, 'so of course she let the paper run out.' One day he brought her home a packet of yellow Post-it notes, which he thought would be useful for her to mark references in books. Next evening, he asked how she was finding them but she said she couldn't make them work. 'Well, how are you using them?' he enquired. 'Well I lick them like this and stick them down . . . look,' she demonstrated, 'but they keep falling off.'

Dinky, whom he adores, flies regularly from the East Coast to visit him as he feels he could no longer tolerate East Coast winters. Just before I visited them they had had a rare disagreement. Bob had referred to her in conversation as 'my step-daughter'. Dinky took him to task: 'You're the only father I've ever known,' she pointed out.

In Dinky's generation other descendants of the sisters, too, have made significant successes of their lives. Debo's son 'Stoker' has been chief steward of the Jockey Club, while her elder daughter Emma is a talented artist and has been for many years the head of National Trust Gardens. Diana's second son Desmond has devoted his life, and financial support, to the Irish Georgian Society, which he founded and which has saved countless eighteenth-century buildings, architectural features and artefacts. He has lectured all over the USA for forty years on the subject. Her son Max is president of the international organisation which governs Formula One motor-racing, and Debo and Diana each has a granddaughter who is a supermodel.

Debo and Diana are the sole survivors of the sisters. Diana celebrated her ninetieth birthday in 2000. When the Temple with its large gardens became too much for her to cope with she sold it, and now lives quietly in her light, airy apartment in the heart of Paris. Her sitting room is at tree-canopy level and over-looks a huge walled garden that once belonged to Napoleon's mother. With the full-length windows open in the summer, it is hard to believe it is only a few minutes' walk to the roar of the Place de la Concorde. Although Diana is very deaf, state-of-the-art hearing-aids enable her to enjoy the regular visits of friends, whom she entertains with customary style and charm, and her large family of grandchildren and great-grandchildren are never far away. Looking back over her life when interviewed for this book she said, 'We all seem to have gone from disaster to disaster, yet I look back on my life, except prison, as being happy, and so lucky.'[25]

Debo is equally family-minded, but for her there is no hint of retirement although her stewardship of Chatsworth is a full-time job that would defeat many a younger person. She still appears to have all the energy and liveliness that so characterized the Mitford sisters, and recently Andrew said in the popular TV series *Great Estates*, 'My wife is far more important to Chatsworth than I am.' This modesty is typical of the Duke. In fact, all the important decisions concerning the running of the estate have always been taken by him, though in recent years he has been assisted in this work by his son, Stoker. In addition, Andrew has taken his position in the county very seriously. Apart from his time as Member of Parliament, he was for a time Mayor of Buxton, and there is scarcely an organization in Derbyshire, large or small, from village cricket clubs to the Mothers' Union and the boards of major public institutions such as hospitals, that has not benefited in some way from his personal support.

But 'the house', as Chatsworth is known locally, has been Debo's responsibility for over fifty years now. The building that had such a hangdog air when the war ended now looks glossy and well cared-for. This has not happened automatically, and the huge cost of running Chatsworth has to be earned by making the house and the estate pay their way. Chatsworth has always been among the leading stately homes in terms of annual visitors, but what impresses those who pay to see it is not just its grandeur – it is one of the great treasure houses of Europe – but the sense that it is a family home and not a museum.[26] Debo cannot understand this, saying that it is a mixture of hotel and museum and that, after all, 'The family do not live in the state rooms.' Nevertheless, she has created an unmistakable ambience of warmth and friendliness, based on what she learned from Sydney. This does not simply apply indoors: the sense of belonging that Andrew and Debo have engendered among the huge staff, some of whom are in the third and fourth generation at Chatsworth and feel they are part of 'the family', permeates everywhere, even to the car parks where Debo's flocks of chickens – especially the stately Buff Cochins – scratching about in the sun have now become almost as famous as the house itself.

With no business training Debo is now a seriously successful entrepreneur, not only overseeing the commercial activities of Chatsworth but for some years serving as a director on the board of an international company where her opinions were greatly valued.[27] From the start she and Andrew were determined to make Chatsworth self-sufficient and it is a matter of personal pride that they have never asked for any government grants. A long-term renovation programme costing half a million pounds per annum concentrates on a major project each year and the work is carried out during the winter months when the house and its hundred-acre garden are closed to the public. When the house is open the full-time staff is supplemented by a small army of local volunteers who enjoy the sense of history of the house and being associated with its treasures. The famous Chatsworth Archive is available to scholars and researchers, and the Duchess is generous in allowing charities to use the house for functions. Several major events, such as country fairs and horse trials, are held annually, attracting tens of thousands of visitors.

When the house was first reopened to the public in the 1950s staff were often asked where they could buy souvenirs so Debo and her housekeeper organized a trestle table to sell matches and postcards. From this small beginning sprang a sizeable trade in souvenirs, books and high-quality items for the home, such as cushions, knitwear, porcelain and hand-made furniture. The famous Chatsworth Farm Shop sells estate produce, and queues form early each morning for new-laid fresh eggs from the Duchess' free-range hens. In recent years a healthy mail-order business has been added, and in the summer of 2000 Debo opened a London branch of the farm shop, which is already as busy as the one on the estate. The half-dozen picnic tables and chairs, originally put out to serve cups of tea to visitors, have evolved into a series of cafés and restaurants, and a highly profitable commercial-catering concern. In the last decade the retail and catering business has increased fifteenfold and Debo now runs a substantial and extremely profitable business, 'And there is no detail of the organization in which Her Grace is not intimately involved,' a member of staff told me. The house, the retail and catering spin-offs now support the estate, rather than the other way round, and it all helps to secure the future of Chatsworth. Debo said recently that she and Andrew 'set out to leave Chatsworth in better heart than we found it'. Without doubt they have succeeded in this aim.

It is this remarkable energy, *joie de vivre* and self-confidence that enabled all the Mitford sisters to take up their own individual causes with such fervour, making their lives so unique that they have now become almost creatures of mythology. If Hitler had never come to power we might never have heard of them outside Society columns or book-review pages, for Nancy was always going to be a writer and Decca, too, was a born wordsmith. Debo and Diana are undeniably able to write well – well enough, certainly, to produce bestselling books – but their writing was a side-dish to the main course of their lives. It was the opposing political forces of Fascism and Communism that lit the tinder of the girls' lives and set alight fires that propelled them from the ordinary to the extraordinary, and made them household names.

And despite the portrait of Sydney promoted by Nancy's books and Decca's account of her unhappy adolescence, it is clear that much of their attitude to life was engendered by their mother, who allowed them freedom to develop while always being there to support in moments of crisis. In reply to his letter of condolence after David's death, Sydney wrote to James Lees-Milne that she thought often of 'the happy days when you were all young and David and I had the children all around us. I was lucky to have those perfectly happy years before the war. Isn't it odd how, when one looks back at that time, it seems to have been all summers?'[28]

SOURCE NOTES

Abbreviations used in citations

CHP	Chatsworth Papers
DD	Deborah, Duchess of Devonshire
DM	Diana Mitford (later Mosley)
DR	Lord Redesdale (David Freeman Mitford)
ER	Esmond Romilly
JLM	James Lees-Milne
JM	Jessica Mitford
NM	Nancy Mitford
OSU	Ohio State University
PJ	Pamela Mitford Jackson
RT	Robert Treuhaft
SR	Lady Redesdale (Sydney Bowles Freeman Mitford)
TM	Tom Mitford
UM	Unity Mitford
VH	Violet Hammersley
YUL	Yale University Library (Beinecke)

Introduction

1 Interview with Lord Longford at the House of Lords, May 2000.
2 Nancy Mitford; Diana Mosley and Unity Mitford. See Bibliography.
3 See Chapter 19.
4 DM to the author January 2001.
5 He was full brother to Caroline Bradley's Cornishman.
6 Rene Wayne Golden, who represented Decca's interests on a number of occasions in respect of screen rights.
7 As a result the film rights to the book (*Straight on till Morning*) were sold but the proposed film was never made. Plans are now in hand by Warner Bros to make a film based partially on the book, with Beryl Markham's memoir *West with the Night*, and other biographical material.
8 Ohio State University, Columbus, Ohio.
9 By US writer/journalist Peter Sussman.

Chapter 1: Victorian Roots, 1894–1904

1 James Lees-Milne, obituary of Sydney, Lady Redesdale; *The Times*, 28 May 1963.
2 'Barty' was probably a contemporary pronunciation of Bertie, although in some contemporary diaries and letters he is referred to as 'Barty'.
3 Redesdale, Sydney, 'The Dolphin' an unpublished memoir, p. 1. Jessica Mitford Papers. OSU/1699.
4 Bowles, Thomas Gibson, *The Log of the Nereid* (Simpkin, Marshall & Co, 1889).
5 Guinness, Jonathan and Catherine, *The House of Mitford* (Hutchinson, 1984), p. 221.
6 Rita Shell, known as 'Tello'. Tello would have several children by Thomas Gibson Bowles. These children were given his name and looked after financially, although he never married their mother. After Sydney and Weenie grew up, and no longer needed

a governess, Tello worked in a senior position at the *Lady* for many years. Sydney was always fond of Tello and knew about her half-brothers.

7   Telephone interview with Julia Budworth, 31 August 2000.

8   *House of Mitford,* p. 186

9   Sydney and her brother George were both painted as children by Millais; it is thought that George was probably the sitter for Millais' *Cherry Ripe,* one of the most popular images in Victorian England and used on the top of many chocolate boxes in the early part of this century.

10 *House of Mitford,* p. 221.

11 *Ibid.*

12 Budworth, Julia, *Never Forget – A Biography of George F. Bowles* (privately published, 2001), p. 182.

13 JM in interview: *Chicago Tribune,* 23 October 1977.

14 Julia Budworth, conversation with the author, 31 August 2000.

Chapter 2: Edwardian Afternoon, 1904–15

1   Interview with Diana Mosley, Paris, 2000.

2   Diana Mosley, letter to the author, 1 August 2000.

3   Guinness, Jonathan and Catherine, *The House of Mitford* (Hutchinson, 1984), p. 230.

4   *Ibid.* p. 154.

5   In her father's book *The Log of the Nereid* (Simpkin, Marshall & Co., 1889), Sydney hardly warrants a mention, but every baby utterance of Weenie is pounced upon and included to illustrate the cleverness and humour of his youngest child. The dedication reads: 'To Captain Weenie (aged 3) whose splendid impatience of discipline and entire want of consideration for others, absolute contempt of elders, complete devotion to her own interests, endeared her to the crew of the Negroid, this book is dedicated by her doting father.' Sydney's grandson, Jonathan Guinness, who has written an excellent biography of his great-grandparents in *The House of Mitford,* told me, 'The key to Sydney is her father.'

6 Mitford, Nancy, *The Water Beetle* (Hamish Hamilton, 1962), p. 8.

7 *House of Mitford*, p. 166.

8 James Lees-Milne, 'Obituary of Sydney, Lady Redesdale', *The Times*, 28 May 1963.

9 OSU: NM to JM, 13 October 1971. Diana and Debo say they never heard this story, and think it 'unlikely'.

10 *House of Mitford*, p. 166.

11 *Ibid.*

12 Governor of the Bank of England from 1920–44, he wielded immense influence in international monetary affairs throughout those troubled decades.

13 See *House of Mitford*, p. 249; also, Mary Soames, *Speaking for Themselves* (Doubleday, 1998), p. 4.

14 *Ibid.*

15 For the full story of the romance between Elizabeth of Austria and Bay Middleton, see John Welcome, *The Sporting Empress* (Michael Joseph, 1975). Captain Middleton broke his neck steeple-chasing in 1892.

16 Blanche confided this secret to Lady Londonderry at Aix where she had gone to be confined. See Lees-Milne, James, *Caves of Ice* (John Murray, 1983), p. 129.

17 Interview with Constancia 'Dinky' Romilly, October 1999. Decca believed that Esmond was Churchill's son. When Giles had a mental breakdown and committed suicide in 1967, Decca said to Nancy that she hoped it didn't run in the family on account of Dinky's children. 'Don't worry about it,' Nancy told her. 'Everyone knows Esmond is Winston's son and the mad streak came from Col. Romilly.' See OSU/1568, JM to DD, 26 October 1995.

18 'Puma': Frances Mitford Kearsey, David's eldest sister, 1875–1951.

19 *House of Mitford*, p. 234

20 *The Water Beetle*, p. 13.

21 The cottage belonged to Lord Lincolnshire. Sydney Redesdale bought it from him shortly after the end of the First World War.

22 Interview with DD, May 2000.

23 David never had an entrenching tool. Diana recalls that they heard as children that Sir Ian Colquhoun had one over his fire which gave Nancy the idea.

24 Duchess of Devonshire, *My Early Childhood* (privately published, 1995), p. 3.

25 Rosemary Bailey and Julia Budworth.

26 Julia Budworth, telephone conversation with the author, August 2000.

27 DD, in conversation with the author, Chatsworth, 2 April 2000.

28 DD, The Mitford Glow', OSU 1710.

29 The late Pamela Jackson, in informal conversation with the author, *c.* 1986.

30 Mitford, Nancy, *The Pursuit of Love* (Hamish Hamilton, 1945), p. 11.

31 *My Early Childhood,* p. 7.

32 Mosley, Diana, *A Life of Contrasts* (Hamish Hamilton, 1977), p. 9.

33 Budworth, Julia, *Never Forget – A Biography of George F. Bowles* (privately published, 2000), p. 155.

34 *House of Mitford,* pp. 155–6.

35 That is, Mosaic Law.

36 The child was Unity. Interview with DD, Chatsworth, May 2000.

37 His grandson, the famous Dr Cyriax of Harley Street, used many of the same techniques.

38 Murphy, Sophia, *The Mitford Family Album* (Sidgwick & Jackson, 1985).

39 Leasor, James, *Who killed Sir Harry Oakes?* (Sphere, 1985), pp. 12–13.

40 OSU/1697, SR to JM, 8 August 1937.

41 *The Water Beetle, p.* 5.

42 Bournhill Cottage on the Eaglehurst Estate (at Lepe, Hampshire), which then belonged to the Marconi family.

43 'They looked identical but talked quite differently', OSU/1565, JM, sundry note.

44 OSU/1697, JM to her parents, September 1926.

45 Duchess of Devonshire, 'Hastings': article in an unidentified magazine.

46 Obituary, Lord Redesdale, *The Times* 26 March 1958, and a subsequent letter to the Editor from Brigadier H.H. Sandilands.

47 Soames, Mary (ed.) *Speaking for Themselves* (Doubleday, 1998), p. 122: Clementine Churchill to Winston S Churchill, 'Helen Mitford dined here 2 nights ago – her baby is 5 weeks old. She is heartbroken that it is not a boy. She is 23 & her hair is grey, which looks so odd with her young face.'

Chapter 3: Nursery Days, 1915–22

1   Last Will and Testament: the Rt Hon. Algernon Bertram, Baron Redesdale, GCVO, KCB.

2   Guinness, Jonathan and Catherine, *The House of Mitford* (Hutchinson, 1984), p. 251.

3   Obituary, Pamela Jackson, *The Times*, 19 April 1994.

4   Butler, Lucy (ed.), *Letters Home* (John Murray, 1991), p. 107.

5   DM, interview with the author, Paris, January 2000.

6   OSU/1701, JM to DR, 9 February 1932.

7   Duchess of Devonshire, *My Early Childhood* (privately published, 1995), p. 7.

8   *Ibid.*, p. 1.

9   *Ibid.*

10 *Ibid.*

11 OSU, MS of 'Mitford Country Revisited', July 1982, p. 3.

12 OSU/1637, JM to DD, 5 March 1990.

13 OSU/1697, PM to SR, 24 June 1925.

14 OSU, Lady Beit (formerly Clementine Mitford) to JM, 13 July 1973.

15 Interview with Rosemary Bailey, Westwell, April 2000.

16 In other words, the appointment of the clergyman.

17 OSU/1637, JM to DD, 28 February 1987.

18 The legend tells of a medieval wedding party where the guests played a game of hide-and-seek. The young bride went off to hide and could not be found though the poor frantic bridegroom tore the house apart. A century later her skeleton was found, clad in the remains of her bridal finery. She had hidden away, curled up in a heavy old wooden chest decorated with the wood of a mistletoe bough; the lid had slammed shut and locked itself.

19 OSU/1565, JM, sundry note, 1 June 1995.

20 See also Murphy, Sophia, *Mitford Family Album* (Sidgwick & Jackson, 1985), pp. 37–8.

21 OSU/1698, SR to JM, 16 May 1968.

22 Mitford, Jessica, *Hons and Rebels* (Victor Gollancz, 1960), p. 13.

23 *Mitford Family Album*, plate.

24 In *Hons and Rebels*, p. 13, Decca says Tom was given the name Tuddemy 'partly because it was the Boudledidge translation of Tim, partly because we thought it rhymed with "adultery"'.

25 *Ibid.*, pp. 13–14.

26 OSU/812, unpublished MS.

27 *Hons and Rebels*, p. 23.

28 DD, interview with the author, Chatsworth, June 2000.

29 *Hons and Rebels*, p. 14

30 Founded by Charlotte Mason in 1887, PNEU has been particularly valuable for military families and those travelling abroad. No matter where the child was taught they could always 'drop back' into the system at whatever level they had reached. Mason founded PNEU because of the widely held belief that 'it was unnecessary to educate girls' and her credo was that 'the child is more complex than the sum of its parts'. Christian ethics is at the base of the curriculum, which concentrates on English and includes maths, science and biology, history and geography, music, dance, art appreciation and play.

31 Mosley, Diana, *A Life of Contrasts* (Hamish Hamilton, 1977), p. 30.

32 *Hons and Rebels*, p. 25.

33 OSU/1928, JM to DD, June 1996.

34 Mitford, Nancy, *Love in a Cold Climate* (Hamish Hamilton, 1949), p. 114.
35 *Ibid.*
36 Lord Longford, interview with the author, House of Lords, May 2000.
37 OSU/1637, DD to JM, undated fax.
38 *Ibid.*, NM to JM, October 1971.
39 *Ibid.*, JM to NM, 13 October 1971.
40 *Ibid.*
41 PRO: Last Will and Testament, Thomas Gibson Bowles, probated 21 March 1922.

Chapter 4: Roaring Twenties, 1922–9

1 Mosley, Charlotte, *Love from Nancy* (Hodder & Stoughton, 1993), pp. 16–17.
2 Acton, Harold, *Nancy Mitford* (Hamish Hamilton, 1975), pp. 14–15.
3 *Love from Nancy*, pp. 16–17, NM to SR.
4 Mitford, Jessica, *Hons and Rebels* (Victor Gollancz, 1960), p. 36.
5 Leslie, Anita, *Cousin Randolph* (Hutchinson, 1985), p. 8.
6 Mitford, Nancy, *The Pursuit of Love* (Hamish Hamilton, 1945), p. 46.
7 YUL, DM to JLM, uncat., 2 July 1981.
8 Hastings, Selina, *Nancy Mitford* (Hamish Hamilton, 1985), p. 46.
9 CHP, Lady Redesdale's housekeeping book, 1934.
10 Lady Kathleen Stanley (née Thynne), married to Oliver Stanley, cousin to the Mitford sisters. Lord Henry Thynne (Viscount Weymouth, heir to Lord Bath, as his elder brother had been killed in the war) had just gone to Oxford. He was responsible for introducing Nancy and the Mitfords to Brian Howard 'and all the others who became our great friends'. DM to author, January 2001.
11 The Countess of Seafield. She stammered badly and was consequently very shy. Brought up in New Zealand, she inherited

several large estates in Scotland, including Cullen and Castle Grant.

12 Acton, *Nancy Mitford*, p. 22.

13 *Hons and Rebels*, p. 10.

14 The rich homosexual son of an industrialist. Later he founded the magazine *Horizon* and employed Cyril Connolly as editor.

15 Duchess of Devonshire, *My Early Childhood* (privately published, 1995), p. 5

16 *Hons and Rebels*, p. 38.

17 OSU/1700, SR to JM, 3 May 1960.

18 *Ibid.*

19 *My Early Childhood*, p. 5.

20 Obituary of Sydney, Lady Redesdale, James Lees-Milne, *The Times*, 28 May 1963.

21 James Lees-Milne, *Another Self* (Hamish Hamilton, 1970), p. 61.

22 *Love from Nancy*, p. 566: NM to Cecil Beaton, 14 May 1969. The unfortunate young man was Mervyn, Viscount Clive, who was killed in the Second World War.

23 *Love from Nancy*, p. 51, NM to TM.

24 OSU/1697, PM to SR, 24 June 1925.

25 *Ibid.*

26 DM, letter to the author, 14 August 2000.

27 CHP, JM to SR, undated, *c.* 1925.

28 OSU/1738, JM to Emma Tennant (niece), 16 October 1993.

29 *Hons and Rebels*, pp. 11–12.

30 Lees-Milne, James, *Ancestral Voices* (John Murray, 1975), p. 444.

31 YUL, DM to JLM, uncat., 2 June 1987.

32 Hastings, *Nancy Mitford*, p. 50.

33 Mosley, Diana, *A Life of Contrasts* (Hamish Hamilton, 1977), p. 47.

34 YUL, DM to JLM, uncat., 19 March 1927.

35 *Ibid.*, 25 March 1927.

36 *A Life of Contrasts*, p. 53.

37 These rules included: 'Must be able to turn two somersaults running forward; Frog jumps across the tennis court; Pass a set of

general knowledge questions etc'. OSU/1698, Book of Hon Rules, sent to JM by SR.

38 DM, interview with the author, Paris, May 2000.

39 *Hons and Rebels*, p. 17.

40 Note from DM to the author, June 2000.

41 *My Early Childhood*, p. 10.

42 *Ibid.*, also DD, interview with the author, at Chatsworth, 4 May 2000.

43 Frederick Lindemann, later Lord Cherwell, 1886–1957. A close friend of Winston S. Churchill, during the Second World War he played a significant role in developing new weapons, and scientific research generally. Later he would become one of the first experts in nuclear physics.

44 Guinness, Jonathan and Catherine, *The House of Mitford* (Hutchinson, 1984), p. 282.

45 *Ibid.*, p. 282.

46 Lees-Milne, James, *A Mingled Measure* (John Murray, 1994), p. 46 and other entries.

47 Lycett Green, Candida (ed.), *John Betjeman Letters* (Methuen, 1990), vol. 1, p. 19.

48 OSU/1633, Bryan Guinness to JM, 13 January 1995.

49 *Hons and Rebels*, p. 39.

50 *Pursuit of Love*, p. 56.

51 *House of Mitford*, p. 279.

52 DM to the author, 16 January 2001.

53 Lees-Milne, James, *Ancient as the Hills* (John Murray, 1997*)*, p. 113.

54 *A Life of Contrasts*, p. 62.

55 Butler, Lucy (ed.), *Letters Home* (John Murray, 1991), p. 107.

56 Guinness, Bryan, *Dairy Not Kept* (Compton Press, 1981), p. 87.

57 *Hons and Rebels*, p. 43.

58 *Ibid.*, p. 44.

59 OSU/1637, JM to DD, 31 March 1982.

60 OSU/1710, DD, 'The Mitford Glow'. It is an exaggeration, of course: there are several letters in which she thanks her mother for new clothes, such as 'the lovely red jumper'.

61 *Hons and Rebels*, p. 16.
62 Like her parents, Diana was married at St Margaret's Church, Westminster. Among the guests were Winston and Randolph Churchill.
63 *A Life of Contrasts*, p. 68.

Chapter 5: Bright Young Things, 1929–30

1 Mosley, Diana, *A Life of Contrasts* (Hamish Hamilton, 1977), p. 70.
2 DM, letter to the author.
3 Butler, Lucy (ed.), *Letters Home* (John Murray, 1991), p. 115.
4 Guinness, Bryan, *Dairy Not Kept* (Compton Press, 1981), p. 89.
5 Mitford, Jessica, *Hons and Rebels* (Victor Gollancz, 1960), p. 48.
6 OSU/1566, JM to DD, 25 August 1990. Stockholm's City Hall was designed by Ragnar Östberg and completed in 1923. It is Sweden's foremost building in the National Romantic style.
7 Described in *Hons and Rebels*, p. 13.
8 OSU, Bryan Guinness file: 'Dichtung und Wahreit among the Mitfords'.
9 Guinness, Jonathan and Catherine, *The House of Mitford* (Hutchinson, 1984), p. 577.
10 Julia Budworth, telephone interview with the author.
11 OSU, Drummonds to JM, 3 July 1929. During research for this book several people have asked, 'Which sister was the one with the "running away account"?' This seems to have struck a chord with many young readers.
12 OSU/1709, JM to NM, 13 October 1971.
13 DM, interview with the author, Paris, January 2000.
14 *A Life of Contrasts*, p. 73.
15 Lees-Milne, James, *Ancestral Voices* (John Murray, 1975), p. 355.
16 *Réalités*,1 June 1961, pp. 71–3.
17 *Hons and Rebels*, p. 35.

18 NM to TM, *c.* October 1928, quoted in Selina Hastings, *Nancy Mitford* (Hamish Hamilton, 1985). Evelyn Waugh had just published *Decline and Fall.*

19 DM to author, December 2000.

20 Evelyn Waugh to Henry Yorke, 20 July 1929, in Amory, Mark (ed.), *The Letters of Evelyn Waugh* (Weidenfeld & Nicolson, 1981), p. 36.

21 *Ibid.* Evelyn Waugh to Harold Acton, July 1929, p. 37.

22 *Hons and Rebels*, p. 14.

23 DM to NM, quoted in Hastings, Selina, *Evelyn Waugh* (Sinclair Stevenson, 1994), p. 219.

24 *Vile Bodies* was published in January 1930. In August that year Waugh published *Labels*, a travel book (the dust jacket was covered in travel labels). Although published after *Vile Bodies* it had been written some years earlier and it, too, was dedicated to Diana and Bryan Guinness.

Chapter 6: The Stage Is Set, 1930–32

1 Lady Redesdale suggested the title 'Our Vile Age' for Nancy's book, which not only reflected her own opinions of present mores, but cleverly made reference to the title of *Our Village*, by a famous eighteenth-century author with the name Mitford. This is a nice example of Sydney's droll humour.

2 Mosley, Charlotte, *Love from Nancy* (Hodder & Stoughton, 1993), p. 62.

3 *Lady*, 10 April 1930.

4 Sir Charles Blake Cochran was a hugely successful theatre impresario, who produced many of Noël Coward's most famous musicals, *This Year of Grace, Bitter Sweet, Cavalcade*, etc., in London. The dancers in his chorus line were known as 'Mr Cochran's Young Ladies', which conferred a distinct cachet. The girls were chaperoned; a high standard of personal behaviour was expected of them and they were subject to dismissal if they married or were suspected of a sexual liaison.

5 Graham, Sheilah, *Beloved Infidel* (Book Club, 1959), p. 115.

6 This is quite true. The Air Ministry imposed conditions for agreeing to Lawrence's wish to remain in the RAF under his assumed name of Shaw. These conditions were that he was not allowed to fly, and he must not speak to any important personages, i.e. 'Churchill, Birkenhead, Sassoon, Lady Astor'.

7 CHP, TM to SR, 17 August 1930.

8 Murphy, Sophia, *Mitford Family Album* (Sidgwick & Jackson, 1985).

9 OSU/155, unpublished MS by JM.

10 Mitford, Jessica, *Hons and Rebels* (Victor Gollancz, 1960), p. 50.

11 OSU/1642, JM to Idden (Ann Farrer Horne) 14 August 1980.

12 OSU/155, Decca on Unity, unpublished MS.

13 *Hons and Rebels*, p. 61.

14 OSU/155, unpublished MS.

15 Pryce-Jones, David, *Unity Mitford – A Quest* (Weidenfeld and Nicholson, 1976), p. 43.

16 OSU/1642, JM to Idden (Ann Farrer Horne), 14 August 1980.

17 *Ibid.*, 22 February 1980. Few people born after 1960 realize the huge impact films had on the previous two generations in terms of manners, dress and accents.

18 OSU/1642, JM to Idden (Ann Farrer Horne), 14 August 1980.

19 Now Lady Soames.

20 Ingram, Kevin, *Rebel* (Weidenfeld and Nicholson, 1985), p. 17.

21 On the other hand Unity was a very unusual girl: her reading was not prescribed and she had been used to the run of an important library since childhood. Perhaps it is not such an odd choice, after all.

22 *Unity Mitford*, pp. 1–2.

23 Mitford, Jessica, *A Fine Old Conflict* (Michael Joseph, 1977), p. 24.

24 OSU/1701.

25 *Ibid.*, various correspondence from JM to DR, 1932.

26 In *The House of Mitford*, Jonathan and Catherine Guinness listed many of the nicknames of the immediate family as a separate section. It covers one and a half pages. See pp. 7–8.

27 Elizabeth Powell (later Lady Glenconner) to David Pryce-Jones, quoted in *Unity Mitford*. Unidentified newspaper article in JM's papers at OSU.

28 Mary Ormsby-Gore, in *Unity Mitford*, p. 53.
29 Garnet, David (ed.), *Carrington, Letters and Extracts from her Diaries* (Jonathan Cape, 1970), p. 473.
30 Mosley, Diana, *A Life of Contrasts* (Hamish Hamilton, 1977), p. 83.
31 May Amende, former maid at Biddesden, in *Unity Mitford*, p. 47.
32 *Daily Telegraph*, 13 April 1994.
33 Lycett Green, Candida (ed.), *John Betjeman Letters* (Methuen, 1990), vol. 1 p. 88.
34 *Ibid.*, p. 101.
35 Hillier, Bevis, *Young Betjeman* (Cardinal, 1988), p. 300.
36 *Ibid.*, p. 102.
37 *Ibid.*, p. 104.
38 *Ibid.*, p. 107.
39 *Ibid.*, p. 95.
40 Maskelyns, a famous stage magician of the twenties.
41 *Young Betjeman*, p. 302.
42 *A Life of Contrasts*, p. 89.
43 Mosley, Sir Oswald, *My Life* (Thomas Nelson, 1968), p. 44.
44 Mosley, Diana, *Loved Ones: Sir Oswald Mosley* (Sidgwick & Jackson, 1983), p. 156.
45 May Amende, in *Unity Mitford*, p. 47.
46 DM to the author 16 January 2001.
47 *A Life of Contrasts*, p. 94.
48 Skidelsky, Robert, *Mosley* (Macmillan, 1981), pp. 338–9
49 *A Life of Contrasts*, p. 94.
50 R.H.S. Crossman, 1961, quoted in *A Life of Contrasts*, p. 96.
51 Webb, Beatrice, Diary *1924–1943* (London School of Economics, 1985), p. 239.
52 Lord Longford, interview with the author, House of Lords, June 2000.
53 *Mosley*, p. 236.
54 Lees-Milne, James, *Another Self* (Hamish Hamilton, 1970), p. 97.
55 Webb, *Diary*, p. 335.
56 Cimmie's mother was the former Mary Leiter, daughter of Levi

Leiter of Chicago. On her marriage Leiter settled £5 million on
Mary, the capital placed in trust for her children.

57 Mosley, Nicholas, *Rules of the Game* (Secker & Warburg, 1982),
    p. 239.
58 DM to the author, January 2001.
59 *Rules of the Game*, p. 217.
60 Lady Pansy Pakenham, in *Unity Mitford*, p. 48.
61 *Rules of the Game*, p. 237.
62 DD, interview with the author, June 2000.
63 Richard Cohen, a present-day fencing expert, maintains that
    Mosley was able to overcome the handicap of his injured foot
    because 'he was very fit and strong'. Letter to the author, 1
    October 2000.
64 DM to the author January 2001.
65 *Rules of the Game*, p. 246.
66 *Love from Nancy*, p. 81.
67 *Ibid.*, p. 82.
68 DM, interview with the author, Paris, 2000.
69 *Loved Ones*, p. 156.

Chapter 7: Slings and Arrows, 1932–4

1   NM to Mark Ogilvie-Grant, 28 March 1931, in Mosley,
    Charlotte *Love from Nancy* (Hodder & Stoughton, 1993), p. 74.
2   Hastings, Selina, *Nancy Mitford* (Hamish Hamilton, 1985), p. 71.
3   Mitford, Jessica, *Hons and Rebels* (Victor Gollancz, 1960) p. 30.
4   *Love from Nancy*, pp. 71–2.
5   OSU/1709, JM to NM, 13 October 1971.
6   *Ibid.*, NM to JM, 18 October 1971.
7   NM to Mark Ogilvie-Grant (undated), in Hastings, *Nancy
    Mitford*, p. 74.
8   Lees-Milne, James, *Ancient as the Hills* (John Murray, 1997),
    p. 158.
9   *Ibid.*, p. 113.
10 *The Times*, 16 June 1933: '. . . In an undefended suit Mrs Diana

Guinness . . . prayed for the dissolution of her marriage with Bryan Guinness on the grounds of his adultery with . . .'

11 NM to Hamish Erskine, 14 June 1933, in *Love from Nancy*, p. 85.

12 *Love from Nancy*, p. 87.

13 Sykes, Christopher, *Evelyn Waugh* (Collins, 1975), p. 41.

14 OSU/1637, JM to DD, 26 April 1985.

15 Violet, sister of Lady Rennell and wife of Edward Stuart Wortley.

16 *Love from Nancy*, p. 90.

17 Hastings, *Nancy Mitford*, p. 86.

18 Mosley, Nicholas, *The Rules of the Game* (Secker & Warburg), p. 248.

19 *Ibid.*, p. 250.

20 Mary Leiter Curzon died in 1906 aged thirty-six, two years after giving birth to her third daughter, Alexandra, from an infection following a miscarriage. Cimmie was aged eight at the time of her mother's death.

21 *Rules of the Game*, p. 252

22 Mosley, Diana, *Loved Ones: Sir Oswald Mosley* (Sidgwick & Jackson, 1983), p. 166.

23 *Rules of the Game*, p. 297.

24 *Ibid.*, p. 258.

25 DM to the author, January 2001.

26 *Rules of the Game*, p. 298.

27 *Ibid.*, p. 259.

28 DM, in conversation with the author, Paris, 2000, and letter, November 2000.

29 Buchan, William, *The Rags of Time* (Ashford, Buchan & Enright, c. 1985), p. 142.

30 Mosley, Diana, *A Life of Contrasts* (Hamish Hamilton, 1977), p. 106.

31 *Ibid.*, p. 107.

32 *Ibid.*, pp. 108–9.

33 BBC2, 2000: *The Age of Nazism – Tourists of the Revolution*.

34 JM to Marge Frantz, 25 May 1986: 'we were forbidden to shave legs (we did it anyway) . . . and wear lipstick . . . why? I suppose

that my parents . . . disliked the idea of trying to attract men by these artificial means.'

35 DR to DM, quoted in Dalley, Jan, *Diana Mosley* (Faber and Faber, 2000), p. 152, and Jonathan and Catherine Guinness, *The House of Mitford* (Hutchinson, 1984), p. 361.
36 *Ibid.*, p. 112.
37 Pryce-Jones, David, *Unity Mitford* (Weidenfeld & Nicolson, 1976), p. 73.
38 NM to DM, in *Love from Nancy*, p. 92.
39 OSU/1701, JM to SR, May 1934: 'I'm so glad you enjoyed your voyage (to Gib) in spite of your thinking it wouldn't be much fun . . .'
40 Mitford, Jessica, *A Fine Old Conflict* (Michael Joseph, 1977), p. 25.
41 OSU/1701, JM to SR, various dates.
42 OSU/1642, JM to Idden (Ann Farrer Horne), 14 August 1980.

Chapter 8: Unity and the Führer, 1934–5

1 Mosley, Charlotte, *The Letters of Evelyn Waugh and Nancy Mitford* (Sceptre, 1996), p. 366.
2 David Redesdale wrote in his copy of this book, against this disclaimer, 'A beastly lie!'
3 Mitford, Nancy, *Wigs on the Green* (Thornton and Butterworth, 1935), p. 16.
4 *Ibid.*, p. 193.
5 *Daily Sketch*, 9 February 1935, but most daily newspapers carried this story.
6 OSU/1567, JM to DD, 14 May 1993.
7 DM to the author, January 2001.
8 Edmund Heines, a senior SA 'Brownshirts' officer.
9 UM to DM, 1 July 1934.
10 Pryce-Jones, David, *Unity Mitford* (Weidenfeld & Nicolson, 1976), p. 86.
11 The two children spent periods at their father's house,

Biddesden. Bryan and Diana remained on exceptionally good terms after their divorce. 'He was always in and out of Eaton Square,' Diana wrote to the author (16 January 2001), 'and I often went to Biddesden to see the little boys when they were not with me. I've got hundreds of letters from Bryan, we became great friends.'

12 Mitford, Diana, A *Life of Contrasts* (Hamish Hamilton, 1977), p. 118.

13 *Ibid.*

14 SR essay quoted in Guinness, Jonathan and Catherine, *The House of Mitford* (Hutchinson, 1985), p. 365.

15 Mitford, Jessica, *Hons and Rebels* (Victor Gollancz, 1960), p. 81.

16 Katz, Otto, *The Brown Book of Hitler Terror and the Burning of the Reichstag* (John Lane, 1933).

17 *Hons and Rebels*, p. 73.

18 Toynbee, Philip, *Friends Apart* (MacGibbon & Kee, 1954), p. 18.

19 JM to DM, 19 January 1935, in *House of Mitford*, p. 367.

20 JM to DR, *ibid.*, pp. 368–9.

21 JM to SR, *ibid.*, p. 369.

22 Michael Burn, telephone interview with the author, July 2000.

23 Diana Mosley's biographer, Jan Dalley, doubts that Hitler did not know of Unity's relationship with Mosley. She believes that Hitler would have had an intelligence dossier on Mosley and Diana, and might have been using Unity and, subsequently, Diana to obtain casual information during their regular fireside chats in the years leading up to the war. On the other hand it is obvious that from this time (the fourth recorded meeting of Unity and Hitler) her family connections were known.

24 22 June 1935.

25 *House of Mitford*, pp. 377–8.

26 *Unity Mitford*, chapter 7.

27 Acton, Harold *Nancy Mitford* (Hamish Hamilton, 1975), p. 78.

28 *Unity Mitford*, p. 127.

29 *Ibid.*, p. 84. However, it should be remembered that Paulette Helleu was never very friendly with either Unity or Diana, and

she never got over her jealousy of the latter's close friendship with her father.

30 Joe Allen, of J.A. Allen and Co. Ltd, publishers, in a private letter to the author, June 2000, and in conversation.

31 *Hons and Rebels*, p. 80.

32 DM to the author, January 2001.

Chapter 9: Secret Marriage, 1935–7

1 Pryce-Jones, David, *Unity Mitford* (Weidenfeld & Nicolson, 1976), pp. 144 and 149.

2 *Ibid.*

3 UM to SR, in Guinness, Jonathan and Catherine *The House of Mitford* (Hutchinson, 1984), p. 378.

4 NM to DM, 18 June 1935, in Mosley, Charlotte, *Love from Nancy* (Hodder & Stoughton, 1993), p. 100.

5 NM to UM, 21 June 1935, in *ibid.*, p. 101.

6 NM to DM, 7 November 1934, in *ibid.*, p. 94.

7 Bernard Shaw, Fabian Lecture: 'In Praise of Guy Fawkes', 1933.

8 Skidelsky, Robert, *Oswald Mosley* (Macmillan, 1975), p. 331.

9 Speech at Ealing, 11 November 1934.

10 OSU/1709, NM to JM, 26 May 1937: Nancy decided not to post this letter, she explained, 'because of my weak mind & not wanting to be tortured when the G[erman]s have conquered us'.

11 Lees-Milne, James, *Prophesying Peace* (John Murray, 1997), p. 444.

12 Mosley, Nicholas, *Beyond the Pale* (Secker & Warburg, 1983), p. 390.

13 Tavener vs Mosley, 1937.

14 DM to the author, November 2000.

15 Dalley, Jan, *Diana Mosley* (Faber and Faber, 2000), p. 196.

16 The villa was at Posillipo, and belonged to Lord Rennell, Peter Rodd's father.

17 Sir Oswald Mosley to DM, in *Beyond the Pale*, p. 366.

18 DM to the author, January 2001.

19 *Beyond the Pale*, p. 364.

20 *Ibid.*, p. 366

21 *Ibid.*

22 Mosley, Diana, *Loved Ones: Sir Oswald Mosley* (Sidgwick & Jackson, 1983), p. 167.

23 Mitford, Jessica, *Hons and Rebels* (Victor Gollancz, 1960), p. 87.

24 CHP, 1935/36, JM to NM, undated.

25 OSU/1566, JM to DD, 11 June 1990.

26 *Hons and Rebels*, pp. 87–8.

27 *Tea at Chartwell, c.* 1928. The picture depicts a scene in the dining room, around which are gathered Thérèse Sickert, Diana Mitford, Edward Marsh, Winston S. Churchill, Professor Lindemann, Randolph Churchill, Diana Churchill, Clementine Churchill and Richard Sickert. It can be viewed at Chartwell, in the studio.

28 *Unity Mitford*, p. 164.

29 Mosley, Diana, *A Life of Contrasts* (Hamish Hamilton, 1977), p. 142.

30 Julius Schaub, Hitler's adjutant and personal assistant.

31 She made visits in January, April, September, and in October for her wedding.

32 *Loved Ones*, p. 172

33 *Diana Mosley*, p. 213.

34 *A Life of Contrasts*, p. 142.

35 FO371/184721.

36 *A Life of Contrasts*, p. 143.

37 *House of Mitford*, p. 384.

38 *Beyond the Pale*, p. 390.

39 *Loved Ones*, p. 168.

40 For most of the details on Derek Jackson I am indebted to *Loved Ones* and the *Dictionary of National Biography*, 1981–5, p. 207.

41 Railway station roughly halfway between Oxford and Cambridge.

42 He won a first-class degree in the natural sciences tripos, part I, in 1926, and a second, in part II, a year later. Leading from this, his work enabled more accurate measurement of hyperfine structures and isotope shifts.

43 The result of Jackson's work, on the hyperfine structure of cae-
sium, was published by the Royal Society in *Proceedings*, 1928.
44 OSU/1709, JM to NM, 13 October 1971.
45 *Prophesying Peace*, p. 444.
46 *Loved Ones*, p. 78.

Chapter 10: Elopement, 1937

1 OSU/1031, ER to JM, 27 June 1940.
2 Unless otherwise cited, I have used Jessica Mitford's *Hons and Rebels* (Victor Gollancz, 1960), chapter 14, for information on her elopement.
3 OSU/155.
4 Toynbee, Philip, *Friends Apart* (MacGibbon and Kee, 1954), p. 92.
5 CHP, JM papers, 1 February 1937.
6 *Ibid.*, 9 February 1937.
7 *Hons and Rebels*, pp. 116–17.
8 CHP, February 1937, and OSU, Esmond Romilly letters.
9 OSU/1697, SR to JM, 23 February 1937.
10 CHP and OSU, NR to SR, 23 February 1937.
11 Duchess of Devonshire, *My Early Childhood* (privately published, 1995), p. 15
12 *News Chronicle*, 13 February 1937.
13 CHP and OSU, JM to SR, 5 March 1937
14 OSU/1674, UM to JM, 3 April 1937.
15 CHP, cable in JM papers, 1 March 1937.
16 *Daily Express*, 1 March 1937.
17 OSU/1697, SR to JM, 3 March 1937.
18 OSU/1674, UM to JM, 3 April 1937.
19 *Ibid.*, Joan Farrer Rodzianko to JM, 4 April 1937.
20 *Ibid.*, Ann Farrer Horne to JM, *c.* 4 April 1937, and 23 April 1937.
21 DD, interview with the author, Chatsworth, May 2000; also Lees-Milne, James, *Ancient as the Hills* (John Murray, 1997), pp. 173–4.

22 OSU, JM to DD, 26 October 1976: 'When you said that my running away . . . was the worst thing in your life I was v. astonished . . . As I remember us in those days we weren't all that adoring . . . I was probably v. jealous of you for being much prettier, and it was far more Boud and me [who were close] . . . Then you also admitted in 1974 when we went over all this that if I had told you about running away you'd have told Muv and Farve, so do admit my instinct . . . was right.'

23 Arthur Pack is a previous subject of the author. See *Cast No Shadow* (Pantheon Books, 1992).

24 OSU/1709, Nancy Mitford file, JM to NM, undated, *c.* 29 May 1937.

25 *Ibid.* Also NM to JM, 14 March 1937.

26 Ingram, Kevin, *Rebel* (Weidenfeld & Nicolson, 1985), p. 151.

27 Now 45 pence, but probably worth the equivalent of £15 in today's terms.

28 OSU, UM to JM, 11 April 1937.

29 Romilly, Esmond, *Boadilla* (Hamish Hamilton, 1937), p. 196.

30 *Rebel,* p. 158.

31 OSU/1674, UM to DM, 16 May 1937.

32 OSU/1709, JM to NM, *c.* early June 1937.

33 OSU/1559, DD to JM, 7 July 1937.

Chapter 11: Family at Odds, 1937–8

1 OSU/1559, DM to JM, 21 May 1937.

2 Gilbert, Martin, *Prophet of Truth* (Heinemann, 1976), p. 911.

3 OSU/1700, SR to JM, 12 June 1937.

4 OSU/1700, SR to JM, 27 March 1960.

5 OSU/1559, combined: DD to JM, 13 June 1937 and 20 June 1937.

6 Guinness, Jonathan and Catherine, *The House of Mitford* (Hutchinson, 1984), p. 410.

7 CHP, SR to JM, 17 June 1937.

8 *Ibid.*

9 *Ibid.*, JM to NM, *c.* early June 1937.

10 OSU/1697, SR to JM, 12 July 1937.

11 OSU/1559, DD to JM, 20 June 1937.

12 *Ibid.*, DD to JM, 30 June 1937

13 OSU/1697, SR to JM, 3 July 1937.

14 OSU/1674, UM to JM, 10 August 1937.

15 *House of Mitford,* p. 415.

16 *Ibid.*, p. 386.

17 Speer, Albert, *Inside the Third Reich* (Sphere Books, 1960), p. 77.

18 FO371/211(97), 27 September 1937.

19 DM, interview with the author, 15 January 2000.

20 Riefenstahl, Leni, *The Sieve of Time* (Quartet Books, 1992), pp. 228–9.

21 Hanfstaengl, Ernst, *Hitler, The Missing* Years (Eyre & Spottiswoode, 1957), p. 224.

22 Ibid., p. 285.

23 *House of Mitford,* p. 387.

24 DM to the author, January 2001. 'Putzi had in fact become rather disloyal. He never stopped telling foreign press chiefs how terrible things were "at the top". E.g. how much Goering and Goebbels disliked each other, and how much both disliked Streicher. He [Putzi] was an inveterate gossip and just the sort of man one doesn't want set loose on hostile foreign journalists. Putzi should have been dropped years before but Hitler kept him on for old times' sake . . . he was a bit of a joke.'

25 *Hitler, the Missing Years,* p. 286.

26 *Ibid.*, p. 289.

27 Mosley, Diana, *A Life of Contrasts* (Hamish Hamilton, 1977), pp. 140ff.

28 Mosley, Nicholas, *Beyond the Pale* (Secker & Warburg, 1983), p. 400.

29 *Ibid.*, p. 399.

30 DM to the author, February 2001.

31 The Acton drawings are now owned by Desmond Guinness and kept at Leixslip Castle in Ireland.

32 Toynbee, Philip, *Friends Apart* (MacGibbon & Kee, 1954), p. 106.

33 *Ibid.*, p. 107.

34 In his diary he says she asked this of a car-park attendant. See Mitford, Jessica, *Faces of Philip* (Heinemann, 1984), p. 32

35 *Ibid.*, p. 112.

36 Ingram, Kevin, *Rebel* (Weidenfeld & Nicolson, 1985), p. 168.

37 OSU, MS by Bryan Guinness, 'Dichtung und Warheit among the Mitfords', *c.* 1959.

38 OSU/1678, JM to NM, 30 November 1968.

39 Later Dame Christian Howard.

40 OSU/1738, JM to Emma Tennant (and others), 3 September 1993.

41 PRO, birth certificate.

42 CHP, JM to DD, 31 May 1937.

43 Mitford, Jessica, *Hons and Rebels* (Victor Gollancz, 1960), p. 148.

44 DM, interview with the author, Paris, 2000.

45 *Hons and Rebels*, p. 149.

46 *Friends Apart*, pp. 115–16

47 DD, interview with the author, Chatsworth, 4 February 2000.

48 Widow of the late Clement Mitford (David's elder brother).

49 OSU/1559, DD to JM, 7 July 1937.

Chapter 12: Slide towards Conflict, 1938

1 Speech by Hitler at Nuremberg, 12 September 1938.

2 A study of statistics available in the Public Record Office shows that prior to 1938 the number of political and criminal prisoners in German concentration camps was approximately 25,000. This was similar to the number of convicted prisoners in modern Germany in 1977. The number confined in 1938 was a marked decrease from that of 1933–4. But even the figure of 25,000 was minute in comparison to the millions confined in Soviet slave-labour camps under Stalin, according to a letter in the *New Statesman* (22 April 1977). This only came to public knowledge two decades later.

3 See Bibliography.

4 Mitford, Jessica, *Hons and Rebels* (Victor Gollancz, 1960), pp. 145–6.

5 Interview notes, Paris, 2000.

6 DM to the author, 16 January 2001

7 Newspaper articles of the day named him as Edward Warburton.

8 Private letter to the author; Mr Allen is an old friend of the author's.

9 *Evening Standard,* 12 April 1937.

10 *The Times,* 2 June 1937, p. 14; *Daily Mirror,* 2 June 1937, pp. 1–2.

11 Guinness, Jonathan and Catherine, *The House of Mitford* (Hutchinson, 1984), p. 412.

12 Quoted in full in David Pryce-Jones, *Unity Mitford* (Weidenfeld & Nicolson, 1976), p. 187. FO/371/21581.

13 DM to the author, January 2001.

14 *House of Mitford,* p. 421.

15 *Ibid.,* p. 417.

16 *Ibid.,* p. 416.

17 *Unity Mitford,* p. 196.

18 *House of Mitford,* p. 417.

19 Cowles, Virginia, *Looking for Trouble* (Hamish Hamilton, 1941), p. 154.

20 *Ibid.*

21 Butler, Lucy (ed.), *Letters Home* (John Murray, 1991), p. 291.

22 Unity did spend Christmas in England. On 15 December a gossip column reported her sitting with her mother, nibbling at a plate of sausages on her lap (Sydney had clearly given up insisting that Unity stuck to Mosaic dietary law), at an Anglo-German Fellowship Christmas party in Bloomsbury.

23 *House of Mitford,* p. 371.

24 Typescript at OSU; partially published in *Forum* (undated).

25 Attallah, Naim, *More of a Certain Age* (Quartet Books, 1993), pp. 50–1.

26 *House of Mitford,* p. 385.

27 Mosley, Diana, *A Life of Contrasts* (Hamish Hamilton, 1977), p. 146.

28 *House of Mitford*, p. 383.
29 Mosley, Nicholas, *Beyond the Pale* (Secker & Warburg, 1983), p. 410.
30 Ravensdale, Irene, *In Many Rhythms* (Weidenfeld & Nicolson, 1953), p. 146.
31 *Ibid.*
32 Hastings, Selina, *Nancy Mitford* (Hamish Hamilton, 1985), p. 115.
33 Nancy also told friends that the 'wicked nanny' had suffered from syphilis and that it may have been passed to her, causing her inability to carry a child. This seems extremely unlikely.
34 OSU, Dr William K. Wallerstein, 5 December 1980.
35 *Hons and Rebels*, p. 152.
36 Toynbee, Philip, *Friends Apart* (MacGibbon & Kee, 1954), p. 122.
37 OSU/1711, Seldon Rodman to JM (undated).
38 *Friends Apart*, p. 154. It seems likely that it was at this point, when things looked very black for the couple, that Decca had her abortion.
39 *Ibid.*, p. 152.

Chapter 13: No Laughing Matter, 1939

1 *NY Daily Mirror*, 'Only Human', 21 April 1937.
2 *Ibid.*
3 *Ibid.*, 20 April 1937.
4 Mitford, Jessica, *Hons and Rebels* (Victor Gollancz, 1960), pp. 209 and 219–20.
5 *Daily Mirror*, 18 March 1937, p. 17.
6 Guinness, Jonathan and Catherine, *The House of Mitford* (Hutchinson, 1984), p. 423.
7 *Ibid.*
8 Pryce-Jones, David, *Unity Mitford* (Weidenfeld & Nicolson, 1976), p. 218.
9 *House of Mitford*, p. 424. Refers to Adolf Wagner, Gauleiter

of Munich. Schwabing is a student and artist district in Munich.

10   *Unity Mitford*, p. 149. Interview with Lady Gainer, widow of the British consul to Munich in 1936. Of the Jews taken to the island on the Danube, Unity told her, 'That's the way to treat them. I wish we could do that in England to our Jews.'

11   DM, interview with the author, Paris, January 2000.

12   *The Times*, 29 May 1940, p. 9.

13   Mosley, Diana, *A Life of Contrasts* (Hamish Hamilton, 1977), p. 160.

14   Trevor-Roper, Hugh (ed.), *Hitler's Table Talk* (Weidenfeld & Nicolson, 1953), p. 631. This conversation took place on the evening of 16 August 1942.

15   DM to the author, 11 November 2000.

16   DM to the author regarding the Hitler photograph, 6 February 2001: 'I still have the receipt (dated June 1940) but I never asked them about it after the war because I assumed the Home Office had probably stolen it. All our bank accounts were examined, and our safe at home forced open. Many things disappeared and our solicitor got apologies, but no more, from the Home Office people . . . One thing they stole was our marriage certificate . . . I had great trouble getting a copy from the ruins of Berlin.'

17   *House of Mitford*. p. 426.

18   *Ibid.*, p. 427.

19   CHP, JM to SR, 23 August 1939.

20   DM to the author, January 2001.

21   OSU/1651, PM to JM, 30 September 1937.

22   NM to SR, 25 May 1939, in Mosley, Charlotte, *Love from Nancy* (Hodder & Stoughton, 1993), p. 113.

23   *Ibid.*

24   *Ibid.*

25   OSU/1651, PM to JM, 19 February 1978.

26   *Love from Nancy*, p. 120.

27   *Unity Mitford*, p. 230.

28   *House of Mitford*, p. 428.

29 *Unity Mitford*, p. 235.

30 *Radio Times*, 11 April 1981, letter from Mr H.W. Koch of York, quoted in *House of Mitford*, p. 432.

31 It was the younger of the two Koch brothers who wrote the letter to the *Radio Times*.

32 *House of Mitford*, p. 434.

33 *Unity Mitford*, p. 236.

34 And, of course, Eva Braun would eventually die with Hitler in a suicide pact.

35 *Unity Mitford*, p. 231.

36 NM to Violet Hammersley, 15 September 1939, in *Love from Nancy*, p. 116.

37 OSU/1697, SR to JM, 29 October 1939.

38 NM to Violet Hammersley, 30 October 1939 in *Love from Nancy*, p. 123.

39 *Ibid.* Also OSU/1651, PM to JM, 30 September 1939.

40 Mitford, Jessica, *Hons and Rebels* (Victor Gollancz, 1960), pp. 196–202.

41 OSU/1679, Blor to JM, 10 December 1939.

42 OSU/1697, SR to JM, 8 December 1939.

Chapter 14: Irreconcilable Differences, 1940–41

1 DD, interview with the author, Chatsworth, 4 May 2000.

2 Mosley, Diana, A *Life of Contrasts* (Hamish Hamilton, 1977), p. 165.

3 Interview at Chatsworth, June 2000.

4 Not Unity's diaries. Janos kept these safely and later sent them to Lady Redesdale.

5 Guinness, Jonathan and Catherine, *The House of Mitford* (Hutchinson, 1984), p. 436.

6 OSU/1697, SR to JM, 28 January 1940: 'I see that doctors today have given up on pills and potions and taken to great mysterious engines, electrical and otherwise. This clinic is full of them and is more like the inside of a battleship than a hospital. She has had all

sorts of electrical tests and X-rays. We are certainly living in a mechanical age.'

7 NM to Violet Hammersley, 7 January 1940, in Mosley, Charlotte, *Love from Nancy* (Hodder & Stoughton, 1993), p. 126.

8 *House of Mitford*, p. 438.

9 A *Life of Contrasts*, p. 167.

10 NM to Violet Hammersley, 10 February 1940, in *Love from Nancy*, p. 130.

11 *House of Mitford*, pp. 439–40.

12 This quote appeared in English papers as 'Unity was always a headstrong girl'. See OSU/1673, TM to JM, 18 January 1940.

13 CHP, JM, to SR, 26 February 1940.

14 OSU/1697, SR to JM, 1 April 1940.

15 *The Times*, 9 March 1940, p. 4.

16 Unless otherwise stated, the information on Decca and Esmond's experiences in the USA is taken from Mitford, Jessica, *Hons and Rebels* (Victor Gollancz, 1960). For the Miami period, see pp. 210–14.

17 OSU/1628, Kay Graham file, 13 April 1978.

18 OSU/1032, Nellie Romilly to JM, 8 July 1940.

19 *Hons and Rebels*, p. 222.

20 Durr, Virginia Foster, *Outside the Magic Circle* (University of Alabama Press, 1990), p. 138.

21 OSU/1029, JM to ER, June 1940.

22 CHP, JM to DD, 17 November 1986.

23 OSU/1697, JM to SR, 22 July 1940.

24 OSU, Jessica Mitford Papers.

25 *Ibid.*

26 *Ibid.*

27 OSU/1020, JM to ER, 8 September 1940.

28 OSU/1031, ER to JM, 11 September 1940.

29 OSU/1029, Max Beaverbrook to Nellie Romilly, 19 November 1940.

30 Mosley, Nicholas, *Beyond the Pale* (Secker & Warburg, 1983), p. 443.

31 Winston Churchill thought this likely. See notes taken at a War Cabinet meeting 28 May 1940, in which Churchill discussed his decision against possible negotiations with Hitler: "'we should become a slave state, though a British Government which would be Hitler's puppet would undoubtedly be set up under Mosley or some such person" . . . no one expressed a flicker of dissent'. See Hugh Dalton, *The Fateful Years* (Frederick Muller, 1957), p. 336.

32 Dalley, Jan, *Diana Mosley* (Faber & Faber, 2000), p. 267.

33 Quoted in TV documentary *Churchill vs. Hitler: The Duel*, Channel 4, 8 May 2000.

34 DM to the author, January 2001.

35 Major Vidkun Quisling, leader of the Norwegian Fascists, proclaimed a puppet government on the day Norway was invaded by the Germans.

36 DM to the author, January 2001.

37 BBC2 programme, 2000, *The Age of Nazism – Tourists of the Revolution.*

38 Skidelsky, Robert, *Mosley* (Macmillan, 1981), p. 447.

39 *Ibid.*

40 Hubert Gladwyn Jebb (later 1st Baron Gladwyn) at the Ministry of Economic Warfare, 1940–42.

41 20 June 1940, in *Love from Nancy*, p. 132.

42 *House of Mitford*, p. 492.

43 *Ibid.*, p. 493.

44 *Ibid.* Jonathan Guinness points out that the statement regarding the profits of the radio station was incorrect. Half the profits were contracted to the German radio company, which was also involved in the venture.

45 DM to the author, January 2001.

46 *A Life of Contrasts*, p. 213.

47 *Ibid.*, p. 189.

48 OSU/1697, SR to JM, October 1940.

49 *Love from Nancy*, p. 139.

50 JM to VH, 1 October 1940, in *ibid.*, p. 140.

51 26 December 1940, in *ibid.*, p. 144.

52 *Ibid.*
53 OSU/1707, NM to JM, 4 July 1940.
54 OSU/1697, SR to JM 26 September 1940.
55 OSU/1700, referred to in JM, to SR, 2 April 1960.
56 3 March 1941, in *Love from Nancy*, p. 147.
57 André Roy was his *nomme de guerre*. His real name was Roy André Desplats-Pilter.
58 Mrs Rattenbury was a murderess.
59 OSU/1559, DD to JM, 6 May 1940.
60 *Ibid.*, DD to JM, 7 October 1940. Joseph Kennedy departed from London on 23 October 1940 at the height of the Blitz saying that he had the greatest respect for Londoners.
61 Lees-Milne, James, *Prophesying Peace* (John Murray, 1997), p. 345.
62 Collier, Peter and Horowitz, David, *The Kennedys* (Secker & Warburg), p. 94,
63 OSU/1679, 'Nannie' to JM, 15 September. Philip Toynbee, Esmond's old friend, was also at Sandhurst at the same time.
64 OSU/1697, SR to JM, 7 October 1940.
65 NM to VH 3 March 1941, in *Love from Nancy*, p. 147
66 *House of Mitford*, p. 581.

Chapter 15: Gains and Losses, 1941–3

1 In *Hons and Rebels* Decca says a nine-bed ward, but in her letters to Esmond she describes it, and draws a diagram of a five-bedded ward.
2 OSU/1648, JM to Anne Horne, 18 October 1984.
3 A Spanish grandee who left her home and family to join the Republicans fighting Franco. See *In Place of Splendour – the Biography of a Spanish Woman* (Michael Joseph, 1940).
4 OSU/1698, SR to JM, 15 April 1941.
5 *Ibid.*, 18 April 1941.
6 Madeau Stewart, interview with the author, Burford, spring 2000.
7 OSU, DD to JM, 1959 (undated).

8   DM to the author, January 2001.

9   Ingram, Kevin, *Rebel* (Weidenfeld & Nicolson, 1985), p. 217.

10 OSU/1030, Virginia Durr to ER, 1 August 1941.

11 OSU/1029, 3 September 1941.

12 *Ibid.*, ER, 6 September 1941.

13 OSU/1030, ER to JM, 11 November 1941.

14 OSU/1031, JM to ER, 1 December 1941.

15 *Ibid.*, Chief of Air Staff to JM (extract), 2 December 1941.

16 Durr, Virginia Foster, *Outside the Magic Circle* (University of Alabama Press, 1990), p. 141.

17 OSU/1029, Wing Commander Ronald Clark, O/C, 58 Squadron Linton on Ouse, York, 4 December 1941.

18 Churchill, Winston S., *The Second World War*, vol. III, *The Grand Alliance* (Cassell, 1950), pp. 539–40.

19 Moran, Lord, *Churchill – The Struggle for Survival* (Constable, 1966), p. 13.

20 Robert Treuhaft, interview with the author, San Francisco, October 1999.

21 OSU/1794, JM notes. Also OSU/1707, Nellie Romilly to SR, 19 March 1942.

22 Pearson, John, *Citadel of the Heart* (Macmillan, 1991), p. 306.

23 OSU, Romilly file, Nellie Romilly to SR, February 1942.

24 OSU/1032, Virginia Durr to SR, *c.* February 1942.

25 Lees-Milne, James, *Prophesying Peace* (John Murray, 1997), p. 349.

26 *Outside the Magic Circle*, p. 141.

27 OSU/1032, Virginia Durr to SR, *c.* February 1942. When Lady Redesdale replied to this she diplomatically repeated several phrases used by Mrs Durr, to let her know, without saying so, that her letter had been safely received.

28 Rosemary, Mrs Richard Bailey, interview with the author, Westwell, March 2000.

29 CHP, JM to SR, 22 February 1942.

30 NM to DM, 22 November 1941, in Mosley, Charlotte, *Love from Nancy* (Hodder & Stoughton, 1993), p. 151.

31　NM to DM, 24 August 1942, in *ibid.*, p. 155.

32　The shop still exists in Curzon Street. Today, a 'blue plaque' commemorates Nancy's association with the building.

33　Lees-Milne, James, *Ancestral Voices* (John Murray, 1975), p. 27.

34　*Ibid.*, p. 26.

35　*Ibid.*, p. 247. Anthony and Christopher, playmates of the Mitford children, were killed early in the war. Timothy's conversion to Roman Catholicism in 1943 while in a PoW camp is said to have distressed the Baileys 'more than the death in action of their two other sons'.

36　*Ibid.*, p. 201. The 'autobiography' became the basis of the novel *The Pursuit of Love.*

37　*Ibid.*, p. 343.

38　*Ibid.*, p. 351.

39　*Ibid., p.* 249.

40　*Prophesying Peace*, p. 312.

41　Hastings, Selina, *Nancy Mitford* (Hamish Hamilton, 1985), p. 144

42　Mitford, Nancy, *The Pursuit of Love* (Hamish Hamilton, 1945), p. 189.

43　Hastings, *Nancy Mitford*, p. 149.

44　*Love from Nancy*, p. 162.

Chapter 16: Women at War, 1943–4

1　Churchill, Winston S., *The Second World War*, vol. III, *The Grand Alliance* (Cassell, 1950), p. 627

2　*Ibid.*, p. 750

3　Mosley, Diana, *A Life of Contrasts* (Hamish Hamilton, 1977), p. 192.

4　*Ibid.*

5　DM, interview with the author, June 2000.

6　*Ibid.*

7　Mosley, Nicholas, *Beyond the Pale* (Secker & Warburg, 1983), p. 483.

8 OSU/1698, JM to SR, 11 April 1943.

9 Mitford, Jessica, *A Fine Old Conflict* (Michael Joseph, 1977), p. 37.

10 OSU 1742, RT to Aranka, 28 December 1942.

11 *Ibid.*, 8 January 1943.

12 *A Fine Old Conflict*, p. 41.

13 *Ibid.*, p. 46.

14 Called 'Mrs Tibbs' in *A Fine Old Conflict*.

15 *A Fine Old Conflict*, p. 46.

16 OSU/1698, JM to SR, 16 March 1943.

17 *Ibid.*, 11 April 1943.

18 Even as an adult Dinky is unmistakably Mitford. I was easily able to identify her from among a jumbo jet-load of passengers when I first met her, merely because I was familiar with photographs of her Mitford aunts at the same age. However, she told me that when she was about nineteen she was walking in New York one day when she noticed a man walking towards her and staring as though transfixed. He passed by, then turned and came back to her. 'I say,' he said in an English voice, 'are you in any way related to Esmond Romilly?' She replied that Esmond was her father. 'Thank God,' he said. 'I thought I was seeing a ghost.'

19 OSU/1698, JM to SR, 11 April 1943.

20 *Ibid.*, 30 May, 1943.

21 *Ibid.*, BT to Aranka, 27 June 1943.

22 Doris Brin Walker, 'Dobbie', interview with the author, San Francisco, 23 October 1999.

23 OSU/1698, JM to SR, 28 June 1943.

24 *Ibid.*, 21 July 1943.

25 *Ibid.*, 22 November 1943.

26 OSU, misc., JM to Winston Churchill, 24 November 1943.

27 *A Fine Old Conflict*, p. 58.

28 When David found this question on forms he always answered, 'Honourable'.

29 Soames, Mary (ed.), *Speaking for Themselves* (Doubleday, 1998), p. 486.

30 *A Life of Contrasts*, p. 198.

31 *Speaking for Themselves*, p. 488.

32 Possibly the development of 'Window', bundles of thin strips of aluminium foil ejected from high-flying aircraft, designed to confuse enemy radar.

33 *A Life of Contrasts*, pp. 199–200.

34 Guinness, Jonathan and Catherine, *The House of Mitford* (Hutchinson, 1984), p. 508

35 OSU/1698, SR to JM, 1 January 1943.

36 *Ibid.*, JM to SR, 27 March 1944.

37 Sally Norton.

38 Kick kept in constant touch with Billy while in Washington. A friend of the author, Quentin Keynes, who worked at the British embassy in Washington, knew her well and used to send their letters through the diplomatic bag.

39 Collier, Peter and Horowitz, David, *The Kennedys* (Secker & Warburg, 1984), p. 129.

Chapter 17: The French Lady Writer, 1944–7

1 James Lees-Milne recorded in his diary that the Duke of Wellington was furious when he heard that Debo had called her son 'Morny', which appeared to be a diminutive of the Wellesley title Lord Mornington. 'How would you like it,' he complained to the Duke of Devonshire at a party, 'if I christened my grandson Harty of Burlington?' Nancy broke in, 'But Debo christened him after her favourite jockey. She's never heard of the Duke of Wellington.' See Lees-Milne, James, *Prophesying Peace* (John Murray, 1997), p. 345.

2 OSU/1698, JM to SR, 15 June 1944.

3 *Ibid.*, 27 March 1944.

4 *Ibid.*, DR to JM, 21 May 1944.

5 *Ibid.*, SR to JM, 16 May 1944.

6 Lord Hartington was killed on 10 September 1944.

7 Patsy White. See Collier, Peter, and Horowitz, David, *The Kennedys* (Secker & Warburg, 1984), p. 144.

8 *Ibid.*

9 *Ibid.*

10 Smith, Amanda, *A Hostage to Fortune* (Viking, 2001), p. 601.

11 NM to SR, 24 September 1944, in Mosley, Charlotte, *Love from Nancy* (Hodder & Stoughton, 1993), p. 167.

12 OSU/1698, SR to JM, 25 July 1944.

13 OSU/1709, NM to JM, 26 May 1944.

14 *Prophesying Peace*, p. 294.

15 Mitford, Nancy, *The Pursuit of Love* (Hamish Hamilton, 1945), p. 193.

16 *Prophesying Peace*, p. 344.

17 *Ibid.*, pp. 348–9.

18 *Ibid.*, p. 355.

19 *Ibid.*, p. 380.

20 *Ibid.*, p. 394.

21 Once part of British India, Burma became a separate state in 1937. Its government continued to function from India after occupation of the country by the Japanese.

22 The information on Major Freeman-Mitford's death is taken from (a) the official Statement of the Company Commander, Devonshire Regiment (OSU 1701) and (b) Commonwealth War Graves Commission records. His grave is at Taukyan War Cemetery, plot 17 F20. See also OSU/1698, SR to JM, 19 June 1945.

23 *Prophesying Peace*, p. 425.

24 Lees-Milne, James, *Deep Romantic Chasm* (John Murray, 2000), p. 101.

25 OSU/1698, SR to JM, 22 April 1945.

26 *Prophesying Peace*, p. 425.

27 *Ibid.*, p. 426.

28 *Ibid.*, p. 460.

29 RT, interview with the author, Oakland, California, October 1999.

30 OSU/1698, JM to NM.

31 OSU/1707, 13 April 1945.

32 OSU/1698, 22 April 1945.
33 NM to EW, 17 January 1945, in *Love from Nancy*, p. 175.
34 Author and publisher, editor of the *London Magazine*, and godson of Mrs Violet Hammersley.
35 NM to SR, 17 September 1945, in *Love from Nancy*, pp. 184–5.
36 NM to Randolph Churchill, 30 September 1945, in *ibid.*, p. 187.
37 John Betjeman to NM, 19 December 1945, in Lycett-Green, Candida (ed.), *John Betjeman Letters* (Methuen, 1990), p. 378.
38 NM to Gaston Palewski, 20 January 1946, in *Love from Nancy*, p. 195.
39 Guinness, Jonathan and Catherine, *The House of Mitford* (Hutchinson, 1984), p. 444.
40 11 February 1947.
41 OSU/1698, SR to JM, 24 March 1945.
42 *Ibid.*, Hasties (Mitford family solicitors) to JM, 15 June 1945.
43 Cockburn, Claud, 'Island Fling', *Punch*, 30 March 1960.
44 *Ibid.*
45 OSU/1698, JM to SR, 21 May 1946.
46 *Ibid.*, SR to JM, 4 February 1946.
47 956 Clayton Street, San Francisco.
48 Extract from RT's address at the memorial for JM held in London.
49 RT, interview with the author, Oakland, California, October 1999.
50 Pele de Lappe, interview with the author, Petaluma, California, October 1999.
51 OSU/1698, JM to SR, *c.* December 1947.
52 CHP, Constancia 'Dinky' Romilly to SR, 27 January 1948.
53 OSU/1709, JM to NM, 16 November 1971.
54 RT, interview with the author, Oakland, California, October 1999.
55 OSU/1709, JM to NM, 13 October 1971.
56 Constancia 'Dinky' Romilly, interview with the author, California, October 1999.
57 OSU/sundry. Transcript of an interview with Jessica Mitford by a TV crew.

58   OSU/1709, JM to NM, 13 October 1971.

59   NM to DM, 19 February 1947, in *Love from Nancy*, pp. 223–4

60   DM to the author, 16 January 2001.

Chapter 18: Truth and Consequences, 1948–55

1   Collier, Peter and Horowitz, David, *The Kennedys* (Secker & Warburg, 1984), pp. 169–71.

2   Guinness, Jonathan and Catherine, *The House of Mitford* (Hutchinson, 1984), p. 443.

3   Pryce-Jones, David, *Unity Mitford* (Weidenfeld & Nicolson, 1976), p. 260.

4   Interview with the author, October 1999.

5   OSU/1698, 26 June 1948.

6   YUL, SR to JLM, 18 June 1948.

7   Lycett-Green, Candida (ed.), *John Betjeman Letters 1926–1951* (Methuen, 1990), pp. 369–70.

8   DM to the author, January 2001.

9   *John Betjeman Letters*. p. 473.

10   Skidelsky, Robert, *Oswald Mosley* (Macmillan, 1975), p. 481.

11   *Ibid.*

12   *Ibid.*, p. 505.

13   Mosley, Diana, *A Life of Contrasts* (Hamish Hamilton, 1977), p. 218.

14   Mosley, Sir Oswald, *My Life* (Nelson, 1970), p. 424.

15   This began a long link between the family and OSU. Alexander Mosley would spend several years at OSU, and by coincidence the papers of Jessica were purchased by the Rare Books and MSS Department, making the college one of the main sources for Mitford researchers.

16   Victor Christian, 9th Duke of Devonshire (d. 1938) represented West Derbyshire from the age of twenty-three in 1891. Edward William Spencer, the 10th Duke (1895–1950) was MP for West Derbyshire from 1923–38.

17   Duchess of Devonshire, *The Estate* (Macmillan 1990), p. xxiii.

18   Increased to seven years in 1968.
19   After an old friend of Debo.
20   Murphy, Sophia, *The Mitford Family Album* (Sidgwick & Jackson, 1985), p. 123.
21   JM to Gaston Palewski, 23 September 1946, in Mosley, Charlotte, *Love from Nancy* (Hodder & Stoughton, 1993).
22   NM to DM, 17 May 1947, in *ibid.*, p. 229.
23   Margot de Gramont.
24   NM to Gaston Palewski, 26 July 1948, in *Love from Nancy*, p. 266.
35   *Ibid.*, 3 June 1949, p. 282.

Chapter 19: Return to the Old Country, 1955–8

1   CHP, JM to SR, *c.* February 1954.
2   *Ibid.*, SR to JM, 28 February 1954.
3   Extract from programme of testimonial dinner given for the Treuhafts in 1985.
4   Mitford, Jessica, *A Fine Old Conflict* (Michael Joseph, 1977), pp. 163–64.
5   *Ibid.*, p. 164.
6   Many years later they fought to obtain a copy of their FBI file through the Freedom of Information Act. Decca said that reading it she could see her old life flashing before her eyes as though she were drowning.
7   *A Fine Old Conflict*, p. 174.
8   OSU, Constancia 'Dinky' Romilly to RT, 21 March 1993.
9   OSU/1629, JM to Kay Graham, 13 March 1979.
10   OSU/1699, SR to JM, 26 February 1955.
11   OSU, RT file, Constancia 'Dinky' Romilly to RT, 21 March 1993.
12   RT, interview with the author, Oakland, October 1999.
13   CHP, JM to SR, 6 August 1955.
14   Mosley, Diana, *A Life of Contrasts* (Hamish Hamilton, 1977), p. 256.
15   OSU/1699, DR to SR, 7 June 1954.

16   RT, interview with the author, Oakland, October 1999.

17   OSU/1698, SR to JM, 26 March 1956.

18   Julia Budworth to the author, 29 May 2000.

19   *A Fine Old Conflict*, p. 183.

20   Pele de Lappe papers, JM to Pele de Lappe, 20 September 1955.

21   Since then the National Trust has changed the arrangements for acceptance of a property, and will only take houses where there is an endowment to ensure adequate upkeep. Also, many National Trust properties are now let at commercial rents to suitable tenants who run the properties partly as family homes. Even so, the difference between an unoccupied National Trust property and an ancestral seat still occupied by the family is marked, e.g. Hardwick vs Woburn.

22   *A Fine Old Conflict*, p. 194.

23   *Ibid.*

24   NM to Raymond Mortimer, 8 September 1955, in Mosley, Charlotte, *Love from Nancy* (Hodder & Stoughton, 1993), p. 407.

25   NM to Evelyn Waugh, 4 August 1955, in *ibid.*, p. 404.

26   *A Fine Old Conflict*, p. 197.

27   19 November 1955, in *Love from Nancy*, p. 410.

28   Decca believed Pam was a lesbian. It is true that Pam shared her home with another woman for a number of years but all the surviving written evidence points to this being a platonic rather than a sexual relationship.

29   OSU, RT file, JM to RT, 12 November 1955.

30   Constancia 'Dinky' Romilly, interview with the author, October 1999.

31   George Gutekunst, interview with the author, Sonoma, October 1999.

32   *A Fine Old Conflict*, p. 203.

33   Reprinted in *The Lively Arts*, date unknown. See transcript of interview in OSU/155.

34   Marge (Frantz), Pele (de Lappe) and Betty (Bacon).

35   OSU/1698, 4 January 1957; about $50,000.

36   NM to SR, 6 September 1952, in *Love from Nancy*, p. 358.

37 *Sunday Times*, 7 March 1954.
38 *Manchester Guardian*, 12 March 1954. See *Love from Nancy*, pp. 381–2.
39 *Ibid.*, p. 369.
40 Hastings, Selina, *Nancy Mitford* (Hamish Hamilton, 1985), p. 225.
41 Mitford, Nancy, *Noblesse Oblige* (Hamish Hamilton, 1956).
42 NM to Hugh Thomas, 15 March 1956, in *Love from Nancy*, p. 412.
43 Sophia Cavendish, b. 18 March 1957.
44 *A Life of Contrasts*, p. 257.
45 OSU/1699, SR to JM, 19 March 1958.
46 OSU/1707, NM to JM, 3 April 1958.

Chapter 20: A Cold Wind to the Heart, 1958–66

1 DM to the author, January 1999: 'my two Guinness sons went to Oxford, Jonathan to Trinity and Desmond to Christ Church – I tell you this in case you think that like us my sons never went to University'.
2 Mosley, Oswald, *My Life* (Nelson, 1970), p. 430.
3 Mosley, Diana, *A Life of Contrasts* (Hamish Hamilton, 1977), p. 240.
4 *My Life*, p. 428.
5 Guinness, Jonathan and Catherine, *The House of Mitford* (Hutchinson, 1984), p. 534.
6 Lord Longford, interview with the author, House of Lords, May 2000.
7 NM to JM, 15 November 1968, in Mosley, Charlotte, *Love from Nancy* (Hodder & Stoughton, 1993), p. 556.
8 NM to Gaston Palewski, 12 June 1958, in *ibid.*, p. 439.
9 OSU/1699, JM to SR, 30 June 1958.
10 RT recalls that the island was valued at $54,000 (about £11,000 then) so he and Decca were able to buy out the other shares for $27,000.

11 Decca had saved every penny she had ever received from the Canadian government widow's pension – even at her most hard-up she had never used it. It was Dinky's college fund.
12 OSU, RT file, JM to RT, 16 April 1959.
13 *Ibid.*, various letters.
14 Mitford, Jessica, *Hons and Rebels* (Victor Gollancz, 1960), p. 228.
15 OSU/RT file, RT to JM, 26 April 1959.
16 RT, interview with the author, Oakland, California, October 1999.
17 *Ibid.*
18 OSU/1746, JM to RT, 15 May 1959.
19 But published in the USA as *Daughters and Rebels*. There was an unexpected boost to sales in the Deep South where it was shelved in bookshops with civil-war materials.
20 OSU, JM to Marge Frantz, 5 June 1959.
21 CHP, JM to DD, 17 August 1959.
22 OSU, JM to RT, 29 July 1959.
23 OSU/1699, 14 October 1959.
24 OSU/1700, SR to JM, 21 April 1960.
25 Rosemary Bailey, Julia Budworth.
26 OSU/100, SR to JM, 10 April 1960.
27 *Ibid.*, 12 August 1959.
28 OSU/1707, NM to JM, 11 March 1960.
29 NM to Heywood Hill (2 letters), 9 and 16 March 1960, in *Love from Nancy*, pp. 446–7.
30 24 May 1960, in *ibid.*, p. 450.
31 RT, interview with the author, Oakland, California, October 1999.
32 *New York Post*, 5 June 1960.
33 19 November 1960.
34 CHP, JM to DD, 11 July 1962.
35 Mitford, Nancy, *The Water Beetle* (Hamish Hamilton, 1962), pp. 6–9.
36 Madeau Stewart was the granddaughter of Tello, Sydney's old governess and confidante. Tello had several children by Tap

Bowles and therefore Madeau was Sydney's half-niece. 'We never spoke of family matters, or the family connection,' Madeau told me, 'although our families were always in touch.' The Stewarts used to rent Sydney's cottage at High Wycombe, for instance, but Madeau was forty before she discovered there was some family connection. Madeau Stewart, interview with the author, Burford, Oxon, 1999.

37 *A Life of Contrasts*, p. 255.
38 NM to Mark Ogilvie-Grant, 14 May 1963, in *Love from Nancy*, p. 488
39 21 May 1963, in *ibid.*, p. 489.
40 OSU/1560, DD to JM, 31 May 1963.
41 OSU/1680, JM to Peter Nevile, 20 November 1991.
42 OSU, Constancia 'Dinky' Romilly to JM and RT, 25 September 1963. Also interview with the author, Oakland, California, 1999.
43 Mitford, Jessica, *The American Way of Death* (Simon & Schuster, 1963), p. 29.
44 OSU/1678, JM to Charlotte Mosley, 4 May 1996.
45 CHP, file, 1963. Cross-reference to JM letter, dated 30 January 1996. See also OSU, JM to RT, 23 June 1964: 'Said he had read my book and for that reason chose the $900 one [casket]. Otherwise would have felt he must get the most expensive, last gesture he could make to his brother etc.' When Bobby Kennedy was murdered Arthur Schlesinger was responsible for making the arrangements when the body arrived at Bethesda. He too recalled Decca's book and chose one of the least expensive caskets, but later agonized about whether he was being 'cheap' or just sensible: 'I remember thinking about how difficult it must be for everybody making that sort of decision.' See his *Robert Kennedy and His Times* (Houghton Mifflin, 1978).
46 The matter did not end with post-publication publicity. Decca began a campaign for inexpensive funerals and with the help of a friend a funeral co-operative was established, which is still active.
47 Mitford, Jessica *Poison Penmanship* (Farrar, Strauss and Giroux, 1979) p. 4.

Chapter 21: Views and Reviews, 1966–80

1 Her husband is Terry Webber.

2 OSU/709, NM to JM, 18 November 1965.

3 OSU/1776, RT file, RT to JM, 31 May 1965.

4 Pele de Lappe papers, JM to Pele, 11 August 1964, and interview with the author, California, October 1999.

5 Letter from Brigid Keenan to the author.

6 NM to DD, 29 March 1969, in Mosley, Charlotte, *Love from Nancy* (Hodder & Stoughton, 1993), p. 562.

7 OSU, JM to DD, 17 July 1969.

8 CHP, JM to DD, 13 May 1969.

9 Pele de Lappe, interview with the author, October 1999; JM to Pele, 26 May 1969.

10 RT, interview with the author, Oakland, California, 1999.

11 NM to DD, 24 October 1969, in *Love from Nancy*, p. 570.

12 OSU/1710, NM to JM, 23 May 1972.

13 CHP, JM to DD, 14 June 1973.

14 OSU, JM to RT, 14 June 1973.

15 OSU/1637, JM to William MacBrian, 30 September 1986.

16 A rare form of cancer, often called Hodgkin's lymphoma because it affects the lymph glands and the body's immune system. Treatment for this condition has now greatly improved and no sufferer would have to tolerate the pain that Nancy did.

17 OSU, JM to DD, 16 April 1994.

18 JM to James Lees-Milne, 24 May 1973.

19 JM to Gaston Palewski, 8 June 1973, in *Love from Nancy*, p. 606.

20 OSU/1712, Joan 'Rudbin' Rodzianko to JM, 5 July 1973.

21 OSU/1710, DD to JM, 8 July 1973.

22 Lees-Milne, James, *Ancient as the Hills* (John Murray, 1997), p. 57.

23 CHP, enclosure with JM to DD, *c.* June 1973.

24 *Ibid.*, JM to DD, 19 September 1974.

25 Pryce-Jones, David, *Unity Mitford* (Weidenfeld & Nicolson, 1976), p. 1.

26 OSU/1561, JM to DD, 25 January 1974.

27 OSU/1361, DD to JM, 11 February 1974.

28 OSU/1642, JM to Idden (Ann Farrer Horne), 23 February 1980.

29 OSU/1651, PJ to JM, 22 September 1976.

30 CHP, 26 October 1976.

31 OSU misc., Clementine, Lady Beit to JM, *c.* November 1976.

32 OSU/1738, JM to Emma Tennant, 24 July 1985.

33 Dalley, Jan, *Diana Mosley* (Faber and Faber, 2000), p. 284.

34 Lees-Milne, James, *Through Wood and Dale* (John Murray, 1998), p. 160.

35 Mosley, Diana, *A Life of Contrasts* (Hamish Hamilton, 1977), p. 264.

36 YUL, DD to JLM, 29 July 1988.

37 Mosley, Diana, *The Duchess of Windsor* (Sidgwick & Jackson, 1980).

38 OSU/1713, Joan 'Rudbin' Rodzianko to JM, 22 September 1980.

39 Lees-Milne, James, *Deep Romantic Chasm* (John Murray, 2000), p. 86.

40 *Sunday Times Magazine*, 'A Life in the Day', DM in interview, November 1983.

41 Guinness, Jonathan and Catherine, *The House of Mitford* (Hutchinson, 1984), p. 553. It is probably fair to say that Myra Hindley, sentenced to life imprisonment more than thirty years ago for her part in the torture and murder of child victims, is the most hated woman in Britain. Lord Longford has campaigned for years for her release on the grounds that she has repented and is a reformed character. Each time this is suggested British newspapers are besieged with angry letters. The Home Secretary has recently stated that for Myra Hindley life means the whole of her life.

Chapter 22: Relatively Calm Waters, 1980–2000

1 Marge Frantz, interview with the author, Santa Cruz, October 1999.

2 In 1977.

3 Decca's record choices included 'The Red Flag' and 'I'm Sex Appeal Sarah', a song she used to sing in Boudledidge to entertain visitors to Asthall.

4 *Sunday Times Magazine*, Julian Jebb, 'The Mitford Sisters', 25 May 1980.

5 Though it was a Raeburn, not an Aga.

6 OSU/1709, NM to JM, 15 November 1968.

7 'The Mitford Sisters'.

8 *The Mitford Girls* (1981) written by Ned Sherrin and Caryl Brahms.

9 OSU/1633, JM to Jonathan Guinness, 10 October 1983.

10 Guinness, Catherine, 'Words with my Aunt, Jessica Mitford', from an unidentified magazine, in JM's scrapbook at her home in Oakland.

11 Interview in JM's scrapbooks, at the Treuhaft home in Oakland.

12 *San Francisco Chronicle*, 21 September 1986.

13 OSU/1637, DD to JM, 2 December 1986.

14 One cannot help wondering if this DVT was caused by the long flight.

15 YUL, DM to JLM, 9 February 1988.

16 OSU/1783, JM to Dobbie Walker, 20 November 1989.

17 *Desert Island Discs*, presented by Sue Lawley, 26 November 1989.

18 *Daily Telegraph*, 27 November 1989, p. 36.

19 Her choice of records was entirely classical, pieces by Mozart, Beethoven and Puccini, a Chopin mazurka and two pieces of Wagner, the '*Liebestod*' from *Tristan and Isolde* and a duet from *The Valkyrie*.

20 OSU/1651, JM to Contancia 'Dinky' Romilly, 12 April 1994.

21 Interview, Oakland, California, October 1999.

22 OSU, Constancia 'Dinky' Romilly to Maya Angelou, 10 December 1994.

23 Dinky was, and still is, a highly qualified casualty nurse in A & E. Interestingly Decca identified Dinky as possessing many of Pam's 'Womanly' qualities even as a small child; see her letters to Sydney in 1941–3.

24 RT's address at the memorial service held for JM in London.

25 DM to the author, 25 February 2001.

26 During one visit to Chatsworth for research the author conducted a mini-census, asking people at nearby tables in the restaurant what had most impressed them. Almost universally they commented on the 'warm and well-cared-for atmosphere – like a family home'.

27 The author's late husband, Geoffrey A.H. Watts, chaired and served on the boards of over sixty companies. He said several colleagues told him that appointing Debo to the board of Tarmac Ltd was the best thing the company had ever done.

28 YUL, SR to JLM, 30 March 1958.

ACKNOWLEDGEMENTS AND CREDITS

During the research for this book I was given a considerable amount of help and assistance by the family, primarily Debo (the Duchess of Devonshire), Diana (the Hon. Lady Mosley), Robert Treuhaft and Constancia 'Dinky' Romilly. I should like to express my immense gratitude to them, and also to the following who have helped in various ways:

Joe Allen, Rosemary Bailey, 'Rab' Bailey, Norman Bell, K.V. Blight (House of Lords Archivist), Julia Budworth, Michael Burn, Ruth Caruth (Beinecke Library, Yale University), Lady Elizabeth Cavendish, Richard Cohen, Betty Colchester Wemyss, Ellen R. Cordes (Beinecke Library, Yale University), Gill Day, Pele de Lappe, Katie Edwards (Decca's secretary), Penny Finchmullen, Marge Frantz, Elva Griffith (Ohio State University), the Hon. Desmond Guinness, Jonathan Guinness (Lord Moyne), George Gutekunst, Janie Hampton, Bevis Hillier, Quentin Keynes, Karen J. Leonard, Lady Elizabeth Longford, Lord Longford, Graeme R. Lovell (advice on inheritance taxes), Mrs J. MacKinnon, Priscilla McWilliams, Helen Marchant (secretary to the Duke and Duchess of Devonshire), Doreen Morris, Charlotte Mosley, the Hon. June Ogilvy, Bernadette Rivett,

Doug Scherer (Ohio State University), Geoffrey D. Smith (Ohio State University), Madeau Stewart, Peter Y. Sussman, Rosemary Taylor, Janet Topp-Fargion (British Library Sound Archive), Sally Toynbee, Michael Waite, Doris 'Dobbie' Walker.

Copyright Acknowledgements

The author wishes to thank the following for their generosity in granting permission for copyright material to be printed in this book, as follows:

Unpublished Material
The Duchess of Devonshire, for quotations from letters by Sydney (Lady Redesdale), Mrs Pamela Jackson, Unity Mitford, and her own unpublished writings, also the unpublished writings of Nancy Mitford and to quote the passage from *Wigs on the Green.*

Diana, Lady Mosley for unpublished and published quotations by herself and Sir Oswald Mosley, and other members of her immediate family.

Robert Treuhaft for quotations by Jessica (Decca) Mitford, himself and Constancia 'Dinky' Romilly.

The Rare Books and MSS Department of Ohio State University, which owns the physical property of Jessica Mitford's papers.

The Beinecke Library at Yale University, which owns the physical property of the James Lees-Milne papers.

Published Material
For quotations from various books (see bibliography for full details of publication):

Desmond Elliott and the Estate of Sir John Betjeman to quote from letters and poetry of Sir John Betjeman.

David Higham Associates for permission to quote from the works of James Lees-Milne.

Hodder & Stoughton for permission to quote from *Love from Nancy*.

Sally Toynbee for permission to quote from *Friends Apart*.

The *Lady* to quote from articles by Nancy Mitford.

Cassell Plc for quotations from *Beloved Infidel*.

Peters, Fraser & Dunlop Group for quotations from the published works of Nancy Mitford: *Love in a Cold Climate*, *The Pursuit of Love*, *The Water Beetle* and *Wigs on the Green*. And from the works of Nicholas Mosley: *Rules of the Game* and *Beyond the Pale*.

The *Sunday Times* for permission to quote from the Julian Jebb article 'The Mitford Sisters'.

The Trustees of the Jessica Mitford Estate for permission to quote from *Hons and Rebels* and *A Fine Old Conflict*.

NB The author has assumed 'fair usage' for quotations of less than 200 words from any publication. Strenuous attempts have been made to contact all copyright holders. In the few cases where it has not been possible to trace assigns and heirs, the author apologizes, and requests that copyright holders make contact through the publishers. Any such notification will be fully acknowledged in future editions of this book.

I should like to sincerely thank those involved in the various production processes of this book. At Little, Brown (London), Richard Beswick, Viv Redman and Hazel Orme. At W.W. Norton (NY), Starling Lawrence, who was responsible for the book's conception. And my literary agent Robert Ducas, who is a never-failing source of support.

Finally, my thanks to David Baldwin, Vanda Hamarneh, Fatie Darwish and Shadi Kabalan ('Song of a Tiger'), who, each in their own way, were of assistance when the page proofs of this book went astray between London and Damascus.

Picture Credits

Devonshire collection, Chatsworth, by kind permission of the
Duchess of Devonshire: 1, 2, 3, 4, 5, 6, 7, 8, 9, 10, 11, 14, 15,
16, 18, 19, 20, 21, 22, 26, 27, 28, 29, 30, 31, 33, 34, 36, 37, 38,
39, 40, 41, 43, 44, 45, 46, 47, 49, 50, 52, 54, 57, 61 (by kind
permission of Desmond Guinness)

OSU: 12, 13, 17, 25, (by kind permission of Robert Treuhaft)

Diana Mosley: 23, 32, 42, 55, 56, 58, 59, 60

Hulton Getty: 24

Associated Press: 35

Popperfoto: 48

Bibliothèque Nationale: 51

Robert Treuhaft: 53, 62, 63

SELECT BIBLIOGRAPHY

All books published in London unless otherwise stated.

Acton, Harold, *Memoir of Nancy Mitford* (Hamish Hamilton, 1975).

Amory, Mark, *Letters of Evelyn Waugh* (Weidenfeld & Nicolson, 1980).

Attallah, Naim, *More of a Certain Age* (Quartet Books, 1993).

Barrow, Andrew, *Gossip* (Hamish Hamilton, 1978).

Boothby, Robert, *I Fight to Live* (Heinemann, 1947).
    Recollections of a Rebel (Hutchinson, 1978).

Bowles, Thomas Gibson, *The Log of the Nereid* (Simpkin, Marshall & Co., 1889).

Bullock, Alan, *Hitler – A Study in Tyranny* (Oldhams Press, 1952).

Butler, Lucy (ed.) *Letters Home: The Letters of Robert Byron* (John Murray, 1991).

Carpenter, Humphrey, *The Brideshead Generation* (Faber and Faber, 1989).

Carrington, Dora, *Letters and Diaries* (Cape, 1970).

Churchill, Winston, *The Second World War,* 5 vols (Cassell, 1948–54).

Collier, Peter and Horowitz, David, *The Kennedys* (Secker & Warburg, 1984).

Cowles, Virginia, *Looking for Trouble* (Hamish Hamilton, 1941).

Dalley, Jan, *Diana Mosley* (Faber and Faber, 2000).

Dalton, Hugh, *The Fateful Years* (Frederick Muller, 1957).

Davie, Mark, *Diaries of Evelyn Waugh* (Weidenfeld & Nicolson, 1976).

Devonshire, Duchess of, *The House* (Macmillan, 1982).
   The Estate (Macmillan, 1990).

Durr, Virginia Foster, *Outside the Magic Circle* (University of Alabama Press, 1990).

Graham, Sheilah, *Beloved Infidel* (Cassell, 1933).

Guinness, Bryan, *Singing out of Tune* (Putnam, 1933).
   Dairy Not Kept (Compton Press, 1981).

Guinness, Jonathan and Catherine, *The House of Mitford* (Hutchinson, 1984).

Halle, Kay, *The Young Unpretender* (Heinemann, 1971).

Hanfstaengl, Ernst ('Putzi'), *Hitler, the Missing Years* (Eyre & Spottiswoode, 1957).

Hastings, Selina, *Nancy Mitford* (Hamish Hamilton, 1985).

Hillier, Bevis, *Young Betjeman* (John Murray, 1988).

Holroyd, Michael, *Lytton Strachey* (Chatto & Windus, 1994).

Ingram, Kevin, *Rebel – The Life of Esmond Romilly* (Weidenfeld & Nicolson, 1985).

Lees-Milne, James, *Another Self* (Hamish Hamilton, 1970).
   Ancestral Voices (John Murray, 1975).
   Caves of Ice (John Murray, 1983).
   A Mingled Measure (John Murray, 1994).
   Ancient as the Hills (John Murray, 1997).
   Through Wood and Dale (John Murray, 1998).
   Deep Romantic Chasm (John Murray, 2000).

Leslie, Anita, *Cousin Randolph* (Hutchinson, 1985).
   The Gilt and the Gingerbread (Hutchinson, 1981).

Lewis, Jeremy, *Cyril Connolly* (Cape, 1997).

Lockhart, Sir Robert Bruce, *Diaries* (Macmillan, 1973).

Lycett-Green, Candida (ed.), *John Betjeman – Letters* (Methuen, 1990).

Mitford, Jessica, *Hons and Rebels* (Victor Gollancz, 1960).
   The American Way of Death (Simon & Schuster, 1963).
   A Fine Old Conflict (Michael Joseph, 1977).

Poison Penmanship (Farrar, Straus and Giroux, New York, 1979).

Kind and Unusual Punishment (Knopf, New York, 1973).

Faces of Philip (Heinemann, 1984).

Mitford, Nancy, *Wigs on the Green* (Butterworth, 1935).

The Pursuit of Love (Hamish Hamilton, 1947).

Love in a Cold Climate (Hamish Hamilton, 1949).

The Blessing (Hamish Hamilton, 1951).

Noblesse Oblige (Hamish Hamilton, 1956).

Don't Tell Alfred (Hamish Hamilton, 1960).

The Water Beetle (Hamish Hamilton, 1962).

Mosley, Charlotte, *Love from Nancy – The Letters of Nancy Mitford* (Hodder & Stoughton, 1993).

Letters of Nancy Mitford and Evelyn Waugh (Sceptre, 1996).

A Talent to Annoy (Beaufort Books, New York, 1986).

Mosley, Diana, *A Life of Contrasts* (Hamish Hamilton, 1977).

Loved Ones (Sidgwick & Jackson, 1985).

The Duchess of Windsor (Sidgwick & Jackson, 1980).

Mosley, Nicholas, *The Rules of the Game* (Secker & Warburg, 1982).

Beyond the Pale (Secker & Warburg, 1983).

Mosley, Sir Oswald, *My Life* (Nelson, 1970).

Murphy, Sophia, *The Mitford Family Album* (Sidgwick & Jackson, 1985).

Nicholson, Harold, *Diaries and Letters*, 3 vols (Collins, 1970).

Powell, Violet, *Five out of Six* (Heinemann, 1960).

Pryce-Jones, David, *Unity Mitford* (Weidenfeld & Nicolson, 1976).

Quennell, Peter, *The Marble Foot* (Collins, 1976).

Ravensdale, Irene, *In Many Rhythms* (Weidenfeld & Nicolson, 1953).

Redesdale, Lord, *Memories*, 2 vols (Hutchinson, 1915).

Romilly, Esmond, *Boadilla* (Macdonald, 1938).

Skidelsky, Robert, *Oswald Mosley* (Macmillan, 1975).

Soames, Mary, *Clementine Churchill* (Cassell, 1979).

Soames, Mary (ed.), *Speaking for Themselves: The Letters of Winston and Clementine Churchill* (Doubleday, 1998).

Speer, Albert, *Inside the Third Reich* (Sphere Books, 1975).

Sykes, Christopher, *Evelyn Waugh* (Collins, 1975).

Trevor-Roper, H.R., *Hitler's Table Talk* (Weidenfeld & Nicolson, 1953).

Toynbee, Philip, *Friends Apart* (MacGibbon and Kee, 1954).

Zeigler, Philip, *Diana Cooper* (Hamish Hamilton, 1981).

INDEX

from Switzerland 305–7; wedding 338–40; first child stillborn 342, 352–3; births of Emma and Peregrine 377, 382, 385; Andrew becomes heir to dukedom 388–9; depicted in *The Pursuit of Love* 395; miscarriages 406, 454; move to Edensor 421–2, 423; and Chatsworth 422–3, 424, 515, 526–8; reunions with Decca 428, 437–8, 440, 494; birth of Sophia 454; visits Kennedy 471; opposition to biography of Unity and dispute with Decca 495–500, 509; protective of family 495–6, 499–500; publishes books on Chatsworth 515; golden wedding 515; and Pam's death 518–19; as entrepreneur 527

Mitford, Diana, *later* Guinness, *then* Mosley: birth 22 (fourth child); appearance 22, 65, 66, 80, 93–4, 130; character 65–6, 477; childhood 23–5, 27–31, 33–5, 37, 41, 43, 44–5, 47–52; education 41, 42, 43, 56; sensitivity to ghosts 44, 126–7; and riding 47; and dancing lessons 53–4; horrified at thought of school or Guides 54; unhappiness and boredom 59, 60, 65, 86, 92; admirers 71, 80, 111; attendance at finishing school in Paris ends in disgrace 79–82, 83–6; visits to Chartwell 83, 91–2; nicknames 85; pet

snake incident 90; prevented from learning German 92; coming out 93–4; engagement to Bryan Guinness 94–5, 97, 98; wedding and honeymoon 99–101; London homes 102–3, 126; early visits to Germany and first contact with Nazis 106–7, 159–62; social life 108–9, 110–12, 127, 130–1; births of Jonathan and Desmond 110, 127; affair with Mosley 131–2, 141–6, 153–7, 164–5, 197–200; growing interest in social conditions 132–3; leaves Bryan 144–6; rift with family over Mosley 145, 150, 157, 198–9, 212, 260, 413; divorce 150, 153–4, 156; and Cimmie Mosley's death 155–7; visits Lord Berners in Rome 162–3; joins Unity in Munich to learn German 174–6; alleged remark on Streicher 191; reaction to *Wigs on the Green* 193–4, 196–7, 212; attends 1935 Nuremberg rally and meets Hitler and Streicher 197; car accident 198, 199; abortion 199–200; secretly marries Mosley in Germany and moves to Wootton Lodge 200–1, 211–12, 213–14, 216; increasing contact with Nazis and meetings with Hitler 204–5, 206–8, 210, 248, 250, 252, 253, 268, 287–9, 321–2, 501; discusses Hitler with Churchill 205; acts as intermediary for BUF's Air Time

Mitford, Unity Valkyrie ('Bobo'), *continued*

sisters 52; education at home 76, 81; trip to Paris 81; pets 90, 109, 125, 206, 308, 382; gives Pam's ring to Hitler 96–7; boredom 106; as skater 114; school attendances and expulsions 116–17, 119–20; closeness to Decca 118, 122, 173, 190, 191, 203–4, 257–8, 260, 283, 412–13; early interest in Fascism 118, 121–2, 140, 159; coming out 124–5, 140; friendship with Rudbin Farrer 124–5; favourite hymn 129; and art school 150; support for Diana 150; joins BUF 156, 157, 163–4; visits Germany and attends first Nazi rally 159–62; finishing year in Germany 166–7, 171–7, 181–9, 202; depicted in *Wigs on the Green* 168–70, 193–4, 197, 212; tries to see Hitler 172, 175–6, 181; reaction to Night of the Long Knives 173; attends Nazi rallies 174; salutes Putsch memorial and embarrasses mother 176–7; first meetings with Hitler 181–7; letter to *Der Stürmer* and subsequent publicity 187–91; anti-Semitism 187–9, 285–6; owns pistol 190; activism in England 190–1, 264–6; chaperoned by father in Munich 192–3; and family cruise 202–4; attacks on 203, 265–6; life in Germany and

developing friendship with Hitler 204–5, 206–8, 231, 244, 247–52; boyfriend 206; reaction to Decca's elopement 228–9, 231, 235, 237; correspondence with Churchill about Austria 242; concern to prevent war 249, 289, 290; extent of relationship with Hitler 250–1, 258, 266, 267–9, 287–8; and Putzi Hanfstaengl's defection 251–3, 284–5; arrested in Prague 266; illness 268–9; relationship with Janos von Almassy 270, 290; writes article for *Daily Mirror* 284; friendship with Erna Hanfstaengl stopped by Hitler 284–5; Hitler arranges flat for 285–6, 290; visit to England (1939) 286; alleged remark to Hitler on London defences 288–9; and onset of war 288–91, 295; threatens suicide if war breaks out 289, 290; refusal to return to England 290; suicide attempt 295–300, 303, 304; reaches Switzerland and brought back to England 304–11; effect of brain damage 311–12, 313, 314, 333–4, 391–2; interest in religion 313, 411; appearance at Debo's wedding leads to questions in parliament 340; recovery 340–1, 377, 389, 391, 411; love of Swinbrook 403; illness and death 411–13; Pryce-Jones's biography causes rift among sisters 494–9